COMPUTER WORLD

Praise for the series:

It was only a matter of time before a clever publisher realized that there is an audience for whom *Exile on Main Street* or *Electric Ladyland* are as significant and worthy of study as *The Catcher in the Rye* or *Middlemarch* ... The series ... is freewheeling and eclectic, ranging from minute rock-geek analysis to idiosyncratic personal celebration — *The New York Times Book Review*

Ideal for the rock geek who thinks liner notes just aren't enough — *Rolling Stone*

One of the coolest publishing imprints on the planet — *Bookslut*

These are for the insane collectors out there who appreciate fantastic design, well-executed thinking, and things that make your house look cool. Each volume in this series takes a seminal album and breaks it down in startling minutiae. We love these. We are huge nerds — *Vice*

A brilliant series ... each one a work of real love — *NME* (UK)

Passionate, obsessive, and smart — *Nylon*

Religious tracts for the rock 'n' roll faithful — *Boldtype*

[A] consistently excellent series — *Uncut* (UK)

We ... aren't naive enough to think that we're your only source for reading about music (but if we had our way ... watch out). For those of you who really like to know everything there is to know about an album, you'd do well to check out Bloomsbury's '33 1/3' series of books — *Pitchfork*

For reviews of individual titles in the series, please visit our blog at 333sound.com and our website at http://www.bloomsbury.com/musicandsoundstudies

Follow us on Twitter: @333books

Like us on Facebook: http

For a complete list of books i

Forthcoming in the series:

Blackout by Natasha Lasky
Faith by Matthew Horton
Moon Pix by Donna Kozloskie
To Pimp a Butterfly by Sequoia L. Maner
I Want You by Derrais Carter
That's the Way of the World by Dwight E. Brooks
Fontanelle by Selena Chambers
Come to My Garden by Brittnay L. Proctor
Nightbirds by Craig Seymour
Come Away with ESG by Cheri Percy
Time's Up by Kimberly Mack
BBC Radiophonic Workshop – A Retrospective by William Weir
Madvillainy by Will Hagle
Beauty and the Beat by Lisa Whittington-Hill

and many more . . .

Computer World

Steve Tupai Francis

BLOOMSBURY ACADEMIC
NEW YORK • LONDON • OXFORD • NEW DELHI • SYDNEY

BLOOMSBURY ACADEMIC

Bloomsbury Publishing Inc
1385 Broadway, New York, NY 10018, USA
50 Bedford Square, London, WC1B 3DP, UK
29 Earlsfort Terrace, Dublin 2, Ireland

BLOOMSBURY, BLOOMSBURY ACADEMIC and the Diana logo are trademarks of Bloomsbury Publishing Plc

First published in the United States of America 2022
Reprinted 2022 (twice), 2023

A catalog record for this book is available from the Library of Congress.

ISBN: PB: 978-1-5013-7898-0
ePDF: 978-1-5013-7900-0
eBook: 978-1-5013-7899-7

Series: 33 1/3

Typeset by RefineCatch Limited, Bungay, Suffolk
Printed and bound in Great Britain

To find out more about our authors and books visit www.bloomsbury.com and sign up for our newsletters.

Contents

Track Listing

Side one

1. 'Computer World' (5:08)
2. 'Pocket Calculator' (4:58)
3. 'Numbers' (3:21)
4. 'Computer World, Pt.2' (3:19)

Side two

1. 'Computer Love' (7:18)
2. 'Home Computer' (6:19)
3. 'It's More Fun to Compute' (4:12)

Computer World Tour 1981–1982 Set List

1. 'Numbers'
2. 'Computer World'
3. 'Metropolis'
4. 'The Model'
5. 'Radioactivity'
6. 'Computer Love'
7. 'Autobahn'
8. 'Neon Lights'
9. 'The Hall of Mirrors'
10. 'Showroom Dummies'
11. 'Trans-Europe Express/Metal on Metal'
12. 'Pocket Calculator'

    ENCORE

13. 'The Robots'
14. 'Home Computer'
15. 'It's More Fun to Compute'.[1]

[1]As Wolfgang Flür noted, 'We adopted the same running order for all of our concerts' (Flür 2000:169).

Kraftwerk's Albums and EPs

Kraftwerk I (1970)
Kraftwerk II (1972)
Ralf & Florian (1973)
Autobahn (1974)
Radio-Activity (1975)
Trans-Europe Express (1977)
The Man-Machine (1978)
Computer World (1981)
Tour de France 12" (1983)
Electric Café (1986)
The Mix (1991)
Expo 2000 EP (1999)
Tour de France Soundtracks (2003)
Minimum-Maximum (2005)

Acknowledgements

As any author knows, writing a book invariably involves many more people than the lone writer churning out prose in isolation. I would like to thank a number of wonderful contributors to the book you hold in your hands today.

Thank you to Bloomsbury and the team at 33 1/3 for choosing to publish the book, particularly Leah Babb-Rosenfeld and Rachel Moore.

Thank you to Emily Mackay for her editorial work on the manuscript. Her suggestions and advice were so helpful and have enhanced the book you now read immeasurably.

Thank you to Bruce Butler for his contributions, his encyclopaedic musical knowledge and for the fact that he seems to have attended every significant gig by every significant band in the last 40 years. You need to write that book, my friend.

Thank you to Steve Mahoney for our daily musical chats. You have the broadest musical taste of anyone I know, and I appreciate your help in reading early drafts of the manuscript and for your ongoing support.

Thank you to Adam Rudegeair for lending your amazing musical prowess and gifts to help me unpack Kraftwerk's genius from a sonic perspective. You are funk brother No.1.

Thank you to the great Emil Schult for your wisdom and insights into the concept of Kraftwerk itself. It has been an honour and privilege getting to know such a creative giant.

Thank you to my children, 'Isi, Ziggy, and Olive for bringing so much joy into my world.

Thank you to my amazing wife Beatriz, who not only encouraged me to follow my passion and write about music, but also edited photos, read multiple drafts of the manuscript and learned to live with my Kraftwerk obsession. Thank you for your unwavering support, my love.

And finally, thank you to Ralf, Florian, Karl and Wolfgang for creating one of the greatest albums of the twentieth century. You certainly presaged the arrival of the computer world in our lives . . .

1
Advancement Through Technology

'We composed the concept of *Computer World* ... and we didn't even have computers at that time. So that was more like a visionary album.'
— *Ralf Hütter, 2008*

Computer World was Kraftwerk's most concise and focused conceptual statement, their most influential record and crowning achievement. *Computer World* transformed the way pop music was composed, played, packaged, and released and, in the process, helped create entire new genres of music including hip-hop, techno, trance, electro, industrial, and synth-pop. They influenced the influencers.

Upon its release on 10 May 1981, the record was a revelation. It was unlike anything created for mainstream consumers of music at that time, an electronic suite of assured and industrious propulsive forward movement. Kraftwerk set off a sonic detonation that is still being felt today.

Computer World represented a major leap forward in its immaculate sound design and sonic construction. The timbre is bright and precise, polished to perfection; music stripped down to its bare essentials, all surfaces glistening with a shiny

Figure 1.1 Computer World album (Photo credit: Steve Tupai Francis).

metallic lustre and precision automation. It was the culmination of many years of experimentation, improvisation, and learning. It is as if Kraftwerk's first seven albums, revolutionary, innovative, and successful though they were, were a dress rehearsal for the flawless sheen that is *Computer World*. The album realized the group's ideal of building a new electronic music from the ground up.

The record was three years in the making (1978 to 1981), produced by the classic line up of Kraftwerk – Ralf Hütter, Florian Schneider-Esleben, Wolfgang Flür and Karl Bartos – in their famed Kling Klang Studio, situated in the industrial heartland of Germany, on the outskirts of Düsseldorf.

The place in which they lived and worked had a direct impact on and correlation with the music they created. The city of Düsseldorf was destroyed during the Second World War, made capital of the new state of North-Rhine Westphalia in Allied-occupied Germany, later West Germany, in 1946, and was completely rebuilt. As Ralf noted: 'It left a vacuum. We are the first post-war generation, and so we are the beginning of something new.'[1] In parallel with the physical reconstruction of Germany, Kraftwerk and their peers took it upon themselves to create a new, positive, rehabilitated, German popular culture as well.

Why Kraftwerk you may ask? Growing up in a beachside suburb at the end of a railway line in Melbourne, Australia in the 1970s and 1980s, you would think it far-fetched that the sounds of four revolutionary creative artists from Germany could reach the ears of a 14-year-old who was eagerly devouring new sounds. And normally you would be correct.

My hometown of Frankston was known as a bit of a dead end, a poor area with high crime rates and low prospects. This was the cliché, the newspaper headline, not the reality. Situated on Port Philip Bay, the town had many sides: the rough end, the million-dollar mansions on Oliver's Hill, and the town centre with its Twin Cinema complex, hub of shops

[1] Aitken 1981.

and recreational outlets. It was also the gateway to the Mornington Peninsula, only 20 minutes' drive down the road, where you could experience forests of pristine beauty, ocean surf beaches and relaxing bay beaches, wineries, and luxury accommodation.

Music was in the DNA of the town. The Pier Hotel, The Grand Hotel: these venues hosted some of the best and brightest Australian bands. The Models. The Go-Betweens. The Triffids. The Church. The Sunnyboys. The Saints. Boys Next Door. Icehouse. Not to mention pub rock stalwarts such as The Angels, AC/DC, Cold Chisel and many, many more. Little did I know at the time, but The Models and Icehouse had followed in the musical footsteps of UK bands like Ultravox!, the Human League and OMD, groups who had been greatly influenced by Kraftwerk.

The Frankston library 'Listening Room' was where it all began for me. In this hallowed space, the walls were lined with row-upon-row of cassette tapes. Vinyl records were available to be played (there were a number of listening stations with headphones), but they were not allowed to be taken out of the library. The compactness and portability of cassettes, though, meant that they certainly were available to be borrowed. And borrow them I did …

The walls were lined with cassettes of all musical descriptions. Classical. Jazz. Mainstream pop. And 'Other'. It is here that I found Kraftwerk. On a fateful day, late in 1981, I came to the library to find some new music. And on that day, I took home two cassettes that would change my life: *Gentlemen Take Polaroids* (1980) by Japan … and … *Computer World* (1981) by Kraftwerk.

Figure 1.2 Computer World cassette (Photo credit: Oliver G).

The significance of *Computer World* was incredible. At this early stage in my life, my musical interests, like those of my peers, had coalesced around mainstream pop and rock bands such as KISS, The Beatles, Blondie, and ABBA. Kraftwerk revealed a totally new form of music, based in electronics, that had a completely different set of sonic parameters and cultural intentions. At the same time, the band's attention to the detail, conceptualisation and delivery of all aspects of their image, packaging, artwork and even liner notes made a huge impression, particularly for an avid consumer of science fiction literature and films. The subject matter of the album too, with its focus on computer games, home computers, and pocket calculators spoke in no uncertain terms to my inner geek.

Computer World opened up a whole new world of musical possibilities that I didn't even know existed, from The Human League, OMD, New Order and Heaven 17 in the UK via Devo, Suicide, and The Residents in the US, to Neu!, Harmonia, Tangerine Dream, and Faust, in Germany.

The simplicity and conceptual completeness of Kraftwerk's vision made it a world you could immerse yourself in as you consumed it. The album made the potentially incongruous and unrelatable concept of a computer world something you could own, that was yours, even in the outer suburban reaches of Frankston.

The comprehensiveness of the album concept and Kraftwerk's precision execution and delivery of the music is so complete that *Computer World* exists as though in its own hermetically sealed universe, as though standing outside of the time and context from within which it was created. I believe this is the essence of the album's longevity and influence among artists and across musical genres. Like a spinning Catherine wheel throwing off sparks in all directions, *Computer World* provided (and continues to provide) an array of revolutionary ideas for artists interested in integrated album design and visuals, new ways of syncopating electronic beats, inventive forms of song construction, rigid structure combined with improvisation, and melodic simplicity and lyrical economy for maximum effect. Kraftwerk had delivered a stunning culmination of all their progression in the 1970s. While very successful upon release, it took a number of years for the album to truly cement its stature as one of the landmark releases of the 1980s. Its reputation continues to grow to this day.

In the chapters that follow, I will outline Kraftwerk's working methods and approach to composition and sound architecture, as well as providing insights into the centrality of their Kling Klang Studio in creating their music. I will also outline the historical, artistic, and geographical influences that shaped their art, including an examination of the cover art and liner notes in detail to help elucidate the *Computer World* concept. Finally, I will analyse each song in depth with a lyrical, musical, and conceptual lens. In this way, I hope to help long-term fans of Kraftwerk, as well as those new to their art, gain some additional insights that may enhance their engagement with what I consider to be one of the greatest records ever made.

2
Painting with Sound

'Except for our voices, there is no member of the group producing direct acoustic sounds. We create loudspeaker music.'
— *Ralf Hütter, 1982*

By the late 1970s, Kraftwerk had engineered and mastered their own process of creation, controlling all elements of production and construction of their music. Kling Klang Studio was fitted out with the best mixing desks and necessary paraphernalia, and they owned the latest electronic equipment. They even had instruments created to aid in their musical endeavours, such as Wolfgang's 'percussion chamber' (used during live performances on the Radio-Activity Tour).[1]

The band were always very secretive about their working methods, restricting access to their studio and creating 'techno-myths' about the equipment they used, making it

[1] The 'percussion chamber' was created by Peter Bollig and was a large cube-like framework of pipes within which the musician stood. It worked using the principle of hand and arm gestures that interrupt light beams, triggering electronic snare, bass, toms and other sounds. Needless to say, it was unreliable when taken on the road and was soon retired (Flür 2000).

hard for other bands to follow their approach or techniques.[2] This only further embellished the (self-perpetuated) image of the band as serious-minded studio boffins in lab coats, going to work each day to experiment and mix new alchemical elixirs in search of musical gold.

The 'boffin' image was something the band cultivated meticulously in interviews. Ralf and Florian would put additional spins and embellishment on it over the years. From their perspective, the band image was that of a collective: individuals were intentionally subsumed within the rubric of the whole, and this included the functional roles of the performers as well. The band members were never referred to as musicians, and their musical roles were usually not spoken of or addressed. In fact, as Ralf noted, they sought to break '... down the barriers between craftsmen and artists, we were music workers'.[3] This was part and parcel of the band's rejection of rock and roll tropes, which tended to focus on authenticity, proficiency, and the 'star performer'. Kraftwerk members all dressed in the same outfits on stage, on the covers of albums, and in publicity shots (until they were replaced by the Kraftwerk robots from 1981 onwards).

Kraftwerk's approach to their deliberately anti-rock image was a form of 'self-effacement ... synthetic rather than authentic' as David Stubbs put it.[4] Rather than using music as an outlet for rock and roll rebellion, Kraftwerk sought to project an image of themselves as European, and later, global

[2] Albeiz 2011b:143.

[3] Dale 2020:22.

[4] Stubbs 2009:107.

citizens, at one with the hum of industry and modernity. Hence their 'business-like' attire and haircuts.

In interviews, band members referred to themselves variously as 'sound engineers' toiling away in their 'electronic garden', craftsmen or artists creating 'a speaker symphony' or 'Electro-Symphony'. As Ralf said: '. . . We play mixers, we play tapes, we play phasers, we play the whole apparatus of Kraftwerk. That's the instrument. Including the lights and the atmosphere'.[5] The band also used artistic analogies such as *musikgemalde* (musical paintings) or 'sound poetry'.

An important element of Kraftwerk's influence and innovation in music was their decision, from 1975's *Radio-Activity* onwards, to avoid traditional acoustic and electric instruments and use electronic instrumentation exclusively. It was a brave decision for a band that was seeking mainstream success in the music industry at a time when condemnation of electronic music among rock critics and purists resulted in histrionic declarations about the death of music as we know it, and disparaging remarks about authenticity.

There were a range of important conceptual and musical reasons for Kraftwerk to go all-electronic, reasons that had everything to do with questioning the orthodoxy and, yes, 'authenticity' associated with certain forms of musical entertainment, privileged over other styles deemed less 'worthy'. Artistically, Kraftwerk's career ambition was to create a new form of musical expression. Ipso facto, in order to do something truly new, you need to let go of what everyone else is doing. Electronic music was a relatively new

[5] Buckley 2015:77.

medium back in the early 1970s. As Wolfgang noted eloquently: '[we wanted] nothing completely influenced by other music styles, cultures, instruments, sounds or countries . . . We had to be our own, self-referential.'[6]

In focusing on electronic music, Kraftwerk were achieving a number of goals at once: they were taking a literal step away from the guitar/bass/drums foundation of rock and roll; they were very obviously innovating and moving in a different direction to most musicians at the time; they were taking ownership of the means of their musical production – producing, composing, creating – in their hermetically sealed Kling Klang Studio environment (in other words, no outsiders needed); and finally, they were making a statement about the conceptual integrity of their musical 'produkt'. As Ralf noted: 'Don't forget in those days successful musicians used important producers to promote and launch their records, but we took on every aspect of the production ourselves.'[7]

Kraftwerk weren't, of course, the first to use electronic sounds and industrial noise, but they sought to downplay the alienating image of this new music. They argued that electronics were 'connecting', 'emotional' and 'sensitive', using the analogy of a heart monitor, which is an instrument, just like a synthesizer, that is sensitive to the beat of one's heart.[8]

While being both excited and repelled by the 'colossal scale and coldness of modern technology',[9] the band noted that they

[6] Flür 2000.
[7] Beecher 1981:1.
[8] Jonze 2017.
[9] Dallas 1975.

wanted to stay on the fence as to judgement of the inherent good or bad of that situation, and crucially, would rather draw 'feelings' from technology. Their conclusion? 'As a result, our music is at the same time impersonal and also very, personal.'[10]

In creating their new sound, Kraftwerk used an array of cutting-edge equipment including synthesizers (Minimoog, ARP Odyssey, EMS Synthi A, Vako Orchestron, Polymoog, Sequential Circuits Prophet-5, Korg PS-3300), voice modulators (Sennheiser Vocoder VSM-201), sequencers

Figure 2.1 Vako Orchestron, originally owned by David van Koevering, founder of Vako (Photo credit: John Ruznak).

[10] Ibid.

Figure 2.2 Mini Moog - Model D (Photo credit: tonetweakers.com).

(Synthanorma), and drum pads and rhythm units (Simmons, Roland), some of which were created by Florian and Wolfgang in collaboration with the band's team of instrument engineers and technicians.

The German instrument manufacturers Matten & Wiechers, from the city of Bonn, were also an integral part of the Kraftwerk operation, syncing their Synthanorma sequencer, which they created for the band, with the Minimoog (according to Wolfgang) in an early pre-MIDI feat of connective-sonic engineering to achieve their dynamic sound. Matten & Wiechers also helped the band achieve the machine-like precision percussion that was a hallmark of their music from *Trans-Europe Express* onwards, via a small CV console they created with six rows of switches hooked up to the Synthanorma, which sequenced and controlled individual percussion sounds.

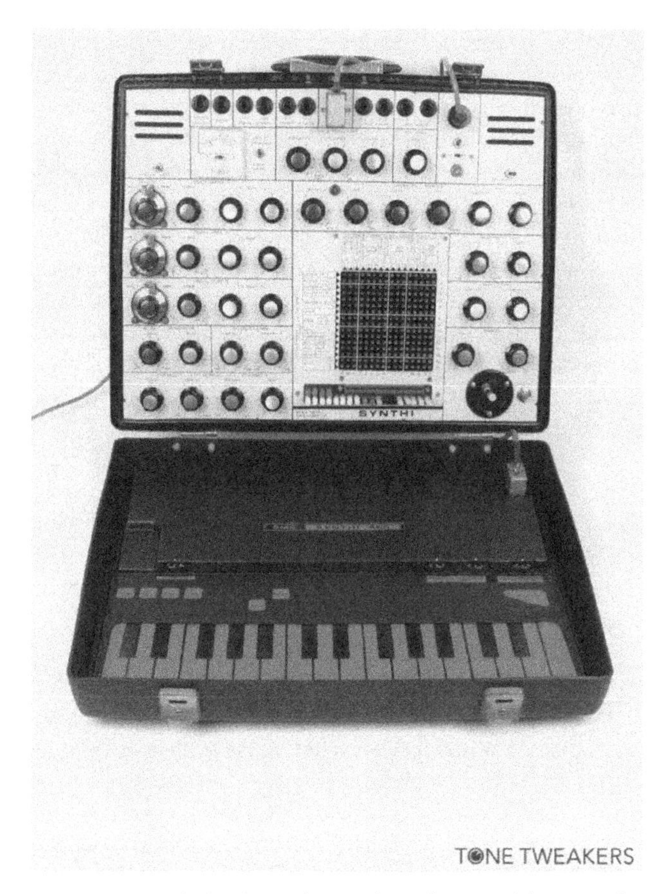

Figure 2.3 EMS Synthi A 'suitcase' synthesizer (Photo credit: tonetweakers.com).

While a precise rhythmic foundation was crucial, improvisation still played a part in Kraftwerk's compositional methods. This is one strand of their music that connects them to the Krautrock/*Kosmiche* experimental tradition of 1960s and 1970s Germany, which was primarily improvised and designed to induce meditative and transcendental states. Krautrock bands like Tangerine Dream, Can, Amon Düül II and Agitation Free, however, stressed cosmic and interstellar outer worlds, while Kraftwerk were always grounded, city-bound and industrial. As Ralf noted in an interview: 'We like to portray the things we do on a day-to-day basis in our music, to relate to everyday technology, such as cars, trains, and other human-controlled machines.'[11]

In composing *Computer World*, the band's overarching principle was *geradeaus*, a German word meaning 'straight ahead'. *Geradeaus* avoids the reductionism associated with words like 'simplistic' or 'minimalistic' carrying with it the idea of knowing where one is going, and wanting to get there as quickly as possible.

When composing music together, one member, often Ralf or Karl, would introduce a melodic riff or coda, and the other members of the band would 'jam' on their synths for several hours. Florian would focus on altering the texture and sound of the music during these sessions.[12] Once locked into a groove they liked, the band would let the sequencers run, sometimes for days at a time, with little change or variation,

[11] Bussy 2005:113.
[12] Ibid:100.

as if to test the riff for musical fitness, like an athlete competing in run-up events prior to the Olympic Games.

These 'laboratory'-tested melodic synth riffs are a trademark of the Kraftwerk sound. In fact, these phrases tend to drift in and out of Kraftwerk compositions and, within the structure of the song, often taking the place of a traditional chorus. This gives the music an ebb and flow, like the gentle lapping of waves on a lake shore at midnight on a full moon. Additionally, the role of voice is crucial to Kraftwerk's music. It is textural (ie, it is another instrument), expressive (ie, Ralf's deadpan intonation is a hallmark of the band's sound) and conceptual (ie, the words spoken deliver the contextual and epistemological meaning of the lyrics on the album). The extensive use of the Vocoder also served to 'equalize' the voice down to the level of other instruments, an effect that the band rejoiced in.[13] This partly reflects their subversive agenda of deconstructing rock cliches along with the auteur theory of the individual star at the centre of creation. As Ralf put it, paraphrasing Warhol, '. . . today, mass production rules . . . Everyone is a star'.[14]

Once they had hit on a piece that suited their purposes, Ralf would transfer it to the sequencer and would then be free to create new melodies or rhythms over the top. This was a technology-enabled methodology (due to the invention of sequencers) that was used in earnest for the first time on *Trans-Europe Express* and *The Man-Machine* and then perfected in all its shiny glory on *Computer World*. As

[13] Gronholm 2011:76.
[14] Ibid: 73.

Wolfgang relates in his autobiography: 'It was an unending cycle of trying out and resetting our electronic slaves.'[15] Their primary aim was to create a sound texture (eg, they focused on the timbre of individual notes, colour of the tone, resonance) rather than song writing and song construction as such. As Ralf put it: 'We spend a month on the sound and five minutes on the chord changes.'[16] John Foxx, the lead singer of the first incarnation of UK band Ultravox! probably put it best when he reflected on what made Kraftwerk special to him: 'Each sound is an astounding sculptural event and is always perfectly placed in its architectural space. You can feel you can walk around those sounds in three dimensions.'[17]

At the end of this process, the band would convene for a listening session, offering critique and approval, discussing the music for hours on end to identify the pieces they liked best. These sections would then be refined, reduced, and sometimes re-recorded.[18] This laborious and unusual procedure of layering melodies and rhythms over a long period of time was complex in construction, yet, like a sauce reduction in fine dining, the result was stunning in its melodic simplicity. Kraftwerk's music is unstoppable in the way the underlying rhythms drone and drill methodically, the repetitive beats lulling the listener into a passive receptive state. It is a hypnotic process. The effect of this intentional

[15] Flür 2000:135.
[16] Beecher 1981.
[17] Buckley 2015:272.
[18] Flür 2000.

structuring of the music is that it directs the listener towards the complex interlocking rhythmic relationships that underpin the music, the core of what makes Kraftwerk special.

Computer World is the most fully realized product of Kraftwerk's compositional methodology – the album is a totally immersive experience in which the texture of the music becomes just as important as the more traditional elements of songcraft in popular music. Startlingly, this was all achieved in a pre-digital world.

A common misconception about Kraftwerk is that they were in the business of prognostication and future-telling. However, as Lynskey noted: 'Kraftwerk were more interested in documenting the present than predicting the future.'[19] Yes, they sang about 'The Robots' and made wry observations about the melding of man and machine. And yes, their decision, after the success of *Autobahn,* to go all-electronic was significant and set them on a separate, innovative, and influential musical path to becoming an 'electronic chamber orchestra' as Ralf told the famous music critic Lester Bangs in 1974. All these innovations combined with the arch, witty, and cohesive art direction provided by Emil Schult, Kraftwerk's artistic director, which referenced both the future and the past so well, meant that it was easy for fans and music critics alike to misconstrue the real focus of the Kraftwerk package.

Kraftwerk's conceptual mandate was really to make futuristic music about the everyday aspects of modern post-industrial life. Even more prosaic than that, their music was

[19] Lynskey 2013.

about the functionality and usefulness for humans of the tools of the post-industrial age in relation to leisure ('Neon Lights', 'The Model' posing for her 'consumer products', 'Computer Love', 'It's More Fun to Compute') and work ('The Man-Machine', 'Computer World'). As Ralf noted: 'Our thing was always to incorporate from everyday life.'[20] Kraftwerk made *alltagsmusik* (everyday music). In this way, they were a contemporary version of Baudelaire's character Monsieur G. from 'The Painter of Modern Life' (1863), a pseudonym for poet Constantin Guys. Baudelaire's essay is about a man who documents the 'passing moment', the seemingly mundane aspects of the modern world, the aspects of change that we don't notice or take for granted. Kraftwerk's focus on the everyday mirrors these notions highlighted by Baudelaire more than a century earlier as the industrial revolution began to take hold. Kraftwerk, to quote Baudelaire, were bent on a similar artistic program, the documentation of a 'music of modern life'.[21]

In line with this philosophy, Kraftwerk also used consumer products in the creation of their music, including computers, which were moving from the military, academic and industrial worlds and onto the retail shelves of department stores and consumer electronics shops. As Ralf explained, Kraftwerk wanted to take computers 'out of the context of those control functions and use them creatively in an area where people do not expect to find them'.[22] Reflecting the

[20] Cunningham 2011:49.
[21] Baudelaire 1863:49.
[22] Toltz 2011:187.

influence of Pierre Schaeffer's musique concrète, Kraftwerk gave these useful everyday gifts of technology, including calculators, translation devices, and toy instruments, new meaning and context on *Computer World*.

This idea connects Kraftwerk to Devo's parallel art music project, which pranked and parodied American consumerism with existential glee and a barely hidden streak of anger and outrage at the excesses of capitalism. Devo viewed crass and commercial consumption through the lens of the corruption of capitalism and ultimately, the downfall of Western civilisation and the human race itself (de-evolution). Conversely, Kraftwerk regarded the products of industrialisation with fondness, affection, nostalgia, and ironic warmth. They were from Düsseldorf after all, the industrial heartland of Germany, the location of the European *Wirtschaftswunder* (economic miracle).

In their focus on technological objects of utilitarian value, Kraftwerk are really investigating and critiquing modernity, and the role of mass culture.[23] The idea of making art out of industry is also latent in the name of the group. *Kraftwerk* is the German word used to refer to power stations. The word can also be broken down to reveal additional implications: *kraft* means power but also denotes energy and dynamics, and *werk* connotes both labour and its employment, as well as an artist's catalogue.[24]

Kraftwerk also saw themselves as specialists who focused singularly on one thing at a time on each album rather than

[23] Cunningham 2011:47.
[24] Anderson 2020:8.

ranging across themes and topics – like manufacturers of stereos who do not want to expand into surround sound television and theatre systems. 'We're not very varied; we zoom in one subject because it's not really song writing. It's more symphonic, the way we write, part of our German musical culture, the orchestral tradition', Ralf told *The Face* in 1982. This approach is an integral part of the success of *Computer World*, a singular conceptual focus allowing an in-depth exploration of the artistic subject which, as a result, still has startling relevance to this day.

Kraftwerk's music and conceptual pre-occupations, while modern and cutting edge on the surface, can actually be placed at the contemporary end of a long tradition of European artistic movements. Magpie-like, they referenced and utilized these traditions for their own artistic purposes. Startlingly for those who critiqued the robotic lack of imagination and artistic skill associated with creating electronic music, *Computer World*, it could be argued, was the culmination of an artistic tradition that includes Da Vinci, Raphael, Beethoven, Wagner, Rodin, and Beuys.

3
Fluxus to Future[1]

'Kraftwerk was a fortunate cooperation and exchange of three cultural individuals [Ralf, Florian and Emil] with emphasis on art, music and technology, reaching for a local, national, international and cosmic expression.'
— *Emil Schult 2020*

Ralf, Florian, Wolfgang, Karl (and Emil) were members of a generation of Germans who regarded the 1960s as a new *Stunde Null* (or Zero Hour, a term that originally referred to 8 May 1945, the end of the Second World War in Europe), a necessary break from the past that rejected the horror, tragedy, and destruction that was Nazism, and the terrible malaise of non-remembering that they and their peers believed their parent's generation had practiced in the post-war reconstruction.

For Kraftwerk's peer group of post-war baby-boomers, atonement, and acknowledgement of the crimes of the past had not been addressed to the extent it should have been by

[1] *Fluxus to Future* is the name of Emil's book documenting his artistic and creative life from the *Kunstakademie* Düsseldorf to the present day.

their parent's generation. 'In the war Germany was finished, everything wiped out physically and mentally. We were nowhere ... We certainly represent the generation with no fathers,' said Ralf.[2] Kraftwerk also rejected the music of their fathers' generation, which was primarily a sickly sweet pseudo-American pop genre known as *schlager*, like Eurovision music on steroids, with overly sentimental, gosh-darn-it-gee-whiz lyrics to document the shallowest emotional life possible.

So, having dismissed their fathers, Kraftwerk instead looked to their grandfathers and grandmothers for inspiration, to the artists and thinkers, musicians and creators of the 1920s and 1930s. The Germany of the Weimar Republic (1919–1933) was their focus: the art, design, and architecture of the Bauhaus movement; the films of Fritz Lang (Metropolis, M) and F.W. Murnau (Nosferatu); and the music of Wagner and Weill. Kraftwerk also took inspiration from movements such as Futurism, Dadaism, and Modernism, as well as later advances in art and music such as Musique Concrète, Fluxus, and Pop Art. Kraftwerk placed themselves in direct lineage with these developments, as Ralf explained: 'Back in the 1920s, people were thinking technologically about the future in physics, film, radio, chemistry, mass transport ... everything but music. We feel that our music is a continuation of this early futurism.'[3]

The music critic, David Toop, once called Kraftwerk the 'pop equivalent of Bauhaus Total Theatre'.[4] This Modernist

[2] Cunningham 2011:45.

[3] Schütte 2020:119.

[4] Toop 2003:119.

movement, founded in 1919 by the architect Walter Gropius, intentionally rejected traditional architectural theory and instead created a modern design aesthetic as a reflection of the new Weimar Republic. It was, in essence, a reform movement, with a vision of changing society by introducing a practical approach to living, blurring the distinction between form and function while integrating elements of art, typography and interior, industrial, and graphic design.

In addition to its homage to the design and typography of the Russian artist El Lissitzky (1890–1941), there is a direct line to Bauhaus in the composition of the cover of *The Man-Machine*. In fact, the shot of the four Kraftwerk members has them positioned (in very stylized and static poses) on a staircase that is reminiscent of the sharp functional canted angles of the staircase in the famous painting by Oskar Schlemmer, *Bauhaustreppe* (Bauhaus Stairway) created in tribute to Gropius and the Bauhaus school.[5]

These ideas and approaches fed directly into Kraftwerk's conception of their own practice. As Ralf explained: 'I see us as the musical Bauhaus ... In their time they could work in theatre, architecture, photography, and short films, but they did not really have the technology to apply their ideas to music; we now have it.'[6]

Just as important to Kraftwerk's philosophy were the Italian Futurists, with their focus on the fetishization of cars, machines, industry, and urbanized living, best exemplified by Filippo Marinetti's 1909 *Manifesto del Futurismo* (Manifesto

[5] Schütte 2020:140.
[6] Bohn 1981.

of Futurism) a modernist tract that posited a renaissance of the arts through a focus on technology. 'Neon Lights' from *The Man-Machine* is Kraftwerk's romantic Futurist/ Bauhausian homage to the beauty and splendour of a functional object in modern life: 'Shimmering neon lights/ And at the fall of night. . . this city's made of light.'

The Kraftwerk sound also had its origins in Futurism and the anti-philosophy of the Dadaists. Luigi Russolo promoted the idea of noise as music and, in 1913, created a tract known as *L'Art dei Rumori* (The Art of Noises).[7] Ralf once said, 'we feel a connection with Futurism and try to build upon the art forms of that period'.[8]

In addition to *Autobahn's* iconic incorporation of the sound of a car engine starting up and driving along the German road network, Kraftwerk simulated the sound of an aircraft dropping its bomb payload on the track '*Von Himmel Hoch*' (From Heaven Above) from their first album *Kraftwerk I*. 'Trans-Europe Express' was based on the recordings the band captured in the field of trains passing by. The song's sister track, 'Metal on Metal' helped give birth to the industrial/electronic body music genre (the likes of Nitzer Ebb, Front 242, and DAF) and was reminiscent of the sound of machines being beaten up.

[7] Yes, the 1980s cult band Art of Noise, produced by Trevor Horn on the ZTT label, who had a hit with 'Moments in Love', were indeed named after the Russolo manifesto. Cool kids, they were.
[8] Schütte 2020:23.

Kraftwerk's obsession with the sound of trains also connects them to Pierre Schaeffer and his *Musique Concrète*. Based at the French radio station *France Musique*, Schaeffer concocted music from found sounds, cutting up magnetic tapes filled with field recordings of disparate sounds and noises. In 1948 he created his first piece, '*Etude aux Chemins de Fer*' (Railroad Study) based on field recordings of trains clattering across the rails.[9] Sound familiar, Kraftwerk fans?

The final piece of the Kraftwerk Avant-Garde art and music influence puzzle is the head of the Darmstadt School, Karlheinz Stockhausen, known as the father of electronic music.[10] As author Uwe Schütte has pointed out, 'Airwaves' from *Radio-Activity* bears a striking resemblance to Stockhausen's *Study I* (1953) and *Study II* (1954). Ralf said: 'We always considered ourselves the second generation of electronic explorers, after Stockhausen.'[11]

The Fluxus movement was an international avant-garde group of artists and composers in the 1960s which also had a big part to play in the Kraftwerk story. These artists shared a common attitude, based in experimental composition and music, asking questions about what could be considered art, introducing a 'do-it-yourself' approach that evolved into conceptual art, 'happenings', performance art, and many other forms.

[9] Reitveld 2011:221.
[10] Iconic Krautrock producer Conny Plank (who produced and engineered Organisation's *Tone Float*, *Kraftwerk I*, *Kraftwerk II* and *Autobahn*) was a studio engineer for Stockhausen early in his career.
[11] Schütte 2020:90.

Founded by George Maciunas in 1960 and named after the art book he edited (*Fluxus 1*) that featured avant-garde musicians such as John Cage, Jon Hassell, and La Monte Young, the most famous proponents of Fluxus include: Dick Higgins, Emmett Williams, Benjamin Patterson, Ben Vautier, Robert Watts, Wolf Vostell, Alice Hutchins, Joseph Beuys and his colleague, Nam June Paik. In popular culture, probably the most well-known Fluxus artist is Yoko Ono.

As Joseph Beuys famously once said: 'Everyone is an artist.' Other elements of Fluxus include the incorporation of humour into art; the intentional employment of randomness, accidents, chance, and happenstance; live performance; encouragement of interaction between audience and artist; questioning of the notion of 'audience' and 'artist'; use of video and film for installations; anti-commercialism and a philosophy of democratisation of art; self-regard as an alternative to galleries and the art establishment; and the use of found objects and whatever is at hand. These were all hugely influential ideas on the art, theatre, and music worlds.

And on Kraftwerk too, with their questioning of the cliches of rock performance, rejection of traditional release schedules, and ownership of their means of production from the creation of their music, concept, marketing, and distribution through to touring. You can see it in small gestures too, like the way, in live performances, they would move to the front of the stage for the encore of 'Pocket Calculator' and encourage the audience to 'press the key to make a little melody'.

Of added significance in our story of Kraftwerk is the fact that Joseph Beuys was appointed Professor of Monumental Sculpture at the *Kunstakademie* (Arts Academy) Düsseldorf. A young student of Joseph Beuys, Nam June Paik, Gerhard Richter, and Sigmar Polke at the Kunstakademie was none other than Emil Schult!

The Creamcheese club was Düsseldorf's equivalent of iconic venues for music and art such as Max's Kansas City (the New York venue associated with the Velvet Underground), CBGB's (the famous New York live venue that was home to Talking Heads, Blondie, Television, and The Ramones), the 100 Club (centre of the London punk scene) and the Blitz Club and Taboo (which birthed the New Romantic movement). Featuring a 20-metre-long bar and a set of 24 televisions, all showing different channels, it was the venue for many of Joseph Beuys' happenings and performances; Ralf, Florian, Wolfgang, Karl, and Emil all attended numerous gigs and exhibitions there. In addition to hosting British bands such as Pink Floyd, Deep Purple, and Genesis, Creamcheese also curated exhibitions by artists such as Andy Warhol.[12]

As Ralf remembers it: 'We were close to the visual arts scene in Düsseldorf, that is very important for Kraftwerk. It was audio-visual music because of the paintings and soundscapes.'[13] The Creamcheese club was therefore a hub for creativity in Düsseldorf, a collision of music and art, with

[12] Ibid:19.
[13] Ibid:20.

musicians and artists intermingling, influencing each other, and spinning off in new directions.

Warhol's influence can be seen very directly in Kraftwerk's visual output. His incorporation of consumer and commercial products into art is mirrored in the use of traffic cones on the covers of their *alltagsmusik* on *Kraftwerk I* (a red-striped traffic cone) and *Kraftwerk II* (a green-striped traffic cone). The concept of Warhol's 'Factory' is reflected in Kraftwerk's Kling Klang Studio. Even the idea of the man-machine and elevating machines is echoed in this quote from Warhol: 'The reason I'm painting this way is that I want to be a machine, and I feel that whatever I do, and do machine-like, is what I want to do.'[14]

In addition to the influence of Warhol, the English conceptual artists Gilbert and George delivered their famous *The Singing Sculpture* performance art piece at the *Kunsthalle* Düsseldorf during which they performed 'Underneath the Arches' for eight hours straight. Gilbert and George could best be described as permanent performance art, living their lives as though participating in a continuous exhibition. With *The Laws of Sculptors* (1969) they constructed a short list of rules by which they set out to live their lives. The two rules most relevant to our discussion of Kraftwerk were: 'always be smartly dressed, well-groomed, relaxed, friendly, polite and in complete control'; and 'make the world believe in you and to pay heavily for this privilege'.[15]

[14] Ibid:24.

[15] Passmore & Proesch 1969.

Figure 3.1 Traffic cone from the cover of Krafwerk II (Photo credit: Steve Tupai Francis).

The Gilbert & George manifesto influenced Kraftwerk in myriad ways, including providing guidance on dress and style, a 'mystification' rather than 'explanation' approach to interviews, control over image and even record release schedules. Not long after witnessing the performance, Florian adopted their sartorial flair as well.

Kraftwerk's ambition was to bring all these disparate influences together. As Ralf said: 'We do everything, and the marriage of art and technology was Kraftwerk right from the beginning.'[16] The phrase they used to describe their art was *gesamtkunstwerk*. It is a term primarily associated with Richard Wagner, denoting an attempt to create a complete work of art bringing different mediums together (opera, dance, theatre, visual arts, music). It was part of Kraftwerk's modus operandi, under the co-ordination of Emil, to create a 'total artwork'.

At the same time, Kraftwerk were consciously and conscientiously seeking nothing less than to create a new German identity, one that encompassed engagement with Europe, valued the arts in all its forms, and acknowledged the pre-Nazi past (nostalgically) while living in the present and heralding the future. For many, *Computer World* was the pinnacle achievement of this goal, delivering Kraftwerk's *gesamtkunstwerk* conceptually and musically.

Computer World also added something new to Kraftwerk's conceptual world building: a global perspective. As will be explored in later chapters, the album introduced themes of change in relation to technology, industry, capital, travel, leisure, and employment that had an international perspective and applicability. This made perfect sense, as Germany and Europe had a major role to play in these transformational societal shifts.

Kraftwerk's favourite film was Metropolis,[17] the famous German expressionist science fiction film (1927) made

[16] Buckley 2015:46.
[17] Flür 2000:135.

during the 'Golden Twenties' of the Weimar Republic, written by Thea Von Harbou and directed by Fritz Lang. In fact, Ralf once said: 'Historically, we feel that if there were a music group in Metropolis, maybe Kraftwerk would have been that group.'[18]

The film is set in a future dystopia in which the benefits and technological delights of the vast Metropolis are enjoyed by only a small class of wealthy industrialists and their families, while in the catacombs, the underground-dwelling workers toil to maintain and drive the great machines that keep the city moving. The film is an essay on bridging the gap of understanding between classes, the nature of work, the means of production, and the dangers and benefits of the relationship between humans and machines. As Maria, the main protagonist, states: 'The mediator of the head and the hands must be the heart.' In other words, it is the Kraftwerk philosophy in theatrical form. The most famous image from Metropolis is that of the robot created by Rotwang, the evil inventor, an idea the band would return to on *The Man-Machine*.

Kraftwerk loved the film so much they even named a song in its honour (Track 3 on *The Man-Machine*). In the film, industry is an expression of human ingenuity; more specifically, the city is the ultimate projection of this idea. It represents both the best and the worst of mankind, an environment in which to work and labour, to live and to socialize.

[18] Schütte 2020:119.

It is the city as an expression of human industry, and work, that is of most interest to Kraftwerk. As Ralf noted: 'Most of the ideas come from our day-to-day experience. We mostly look at our work and ourselves, things we talk about, things we understand, because we live with them.'[19] In Kraftwerk's (computer) world, Kling Klang Studio was their place of work, the location of their creative labours, their private city, their own Metropolis, constructed to produce their Kling Klang Produkt. David Bowie picked up on the theme in an interview for *Rolling Stone* in 1976, telling the magazine that Kraftwerk were his favourite group and that they play 'noise music to increase productivity'.[20]

Computer World is partly a meditation on the changing nature of work and labour. Technology was just beginning to question the separation of workplace from home. Portable computing, particularly laptops, and eventually mobile phones and other miniaturisation technologies, would lead to the breakdown of this artificial separation. Today, a café is a place of work, the home is a place of work, and the workplace can be a place of leisure (just ask anyone who has been to Facebook's Menlo Park facility or visited the Googleplex Campus).[21]

All these disparate cultural, musical, artistic, architectural and societal influences had informed Kraftwerk's practice from their early records and into their mid-to-late 1970s imperial phase. It could also be argued though, that on these

[19] Pattie 2011:124.
[20] Crowe 1976.
[21] Pattie 2011:133.

(wonderful) records, Kraftwerk's very deliberate intent to emphasize a German identity within a pan-European context revealed their influences, deliberately, yet subtly, to those who knew what to look for. On *Computer World*, however, by elevating their focus to a global perspective, the band ensured their work had, for the first time, a truly global appeal.

4
Kling Klang Produkt

'I've always attempted to contribute to electronic music in whatever way I was capable—be it by providing images, lyrics, or crafting objects. But the bottom line was always: how can I contribute to civilization?'
— *Emil Schult, 2013*

This chapter will focus on the art and design of the *Computer World* cover, the inner sleeve, and the liner notes.

The famous front cover of *Computer World*[1] was created by Emil Schult, Kraftwerk's very own fifth Beatle. As he would do with many of the band members and collaborators of Kraftwerk over the years, it was Florian who introduced Emil to the band one day, having seen his comic book illustrations: 'When I met Emil, and when he showed his comics to me, I thought they looked like our music.'[2]

Emil was born in Dessau in 1946, although he spent much time abroad in his formative years, attending high school in

[1] The back cover and inner sleeve photos were shot by frequent Kraftwerk collaborator, Günter Fröhling.
[2] Buckley 2015:119.

the United States. He visited the World's Fair in New York in 1964 and was particularly stunned by the *Futurama II* exhibit, where he heard early synthesizers and electronic instruments, created by Raymond Scott, for the first time. As Emil relayed, he was confronted by 'sounds that sounded as if they came directly from the future. The illusion was perfect . . . For me, electronic music was the soundtrack to the future as we Westerners imagined it.'[3]

Emil became centrally important to Kraftwerk's conceptual endeavours. He would eventually live at 9 Berger Allee in Düsseldorf with Karl and Wolfgang. As Emil himself said: 'I had an influence on everything.'[4] The band's nickname for him was 'vibrations manager'.[5] Wolfgang called him the 'guru'. Ralf thought of him as the band's 'medium'. Emil also understood the Kraftwerk *gesamtkunstwerk* at a fundamental level. For him, music and image were the two main 'meta-languages' of the universe.

To say Emil could multitask would be an understatement. He facilitated an artistic dialogue within the band in his role as Kraftwerk's in-house art director, driving and overseeing the band's visual identity creating, in the process, three of their most iconic record covers (*Autobahn*, *Radio-Activity* and *Computer World*). He wrote and illustrated the comic that was included with early copies of *Ralf and Florian*, and he conceptualized the neon signs with the band member's

[3] Schult 2013.
[4] Buckley 2015:49.
[5] Schütte 2020:232.

Figure 4.1 Emil Schult creating Computer World painting (Photo credit: Emil Schult).

names on them that first made an appearance on the back cover of that album. He did the lighting for early Kraftwerk gigs as well.

As a fluent English speaker, Emil wrote lyrics for many of Kraftwerk's songs. In addition to 'Computer World', 'Pocket Calculator', and 'Computer Love' on *Computer World*, he

Figure 4.2 Emil Schult creating Computer World painting (Photo credit: Emil Schult).

contributed to the lyrics for 'Trans-Europe Express', 'The Hall of Mirrors', 'The Model', 'Autobahn', 'Radio-Activity', and many others.

In the early days after he joined the Kraftwerk team, Emil played guitar and violin when the band played live (in the period between *Ralf and Florian* and *Autobahn*). He was eventually replaced by short-lived Kraftwerk member Klaus Roeder in that musical role. Emil took this all in his stride with due humility. In fact, when Wolfgang joined the band, Emil had to airbrush himself out of the original painting for the front cover of Autobahn, replacing his head with Wolfgang's. Emil can still be seen in the rear-view mirror among the other members of the band.

Emil also played a practical and logistical role in the band. He was the tour manager for the world tour of *Computer World*, organising logistics, looking after the band members, ensuring the stage set was moved from place to place, unpacked, set up, and bumped out of each venue. It was Emil who suggested the idea of making films to project during Kraftwerk concerts. He helped with the development and redesign of instruments, producing visual representations and schematics of the band's ideas. He also participated in band interviews. Well versed in working in any medium for any task, Emil was the living embodiment of Kraftwerk's conceptual approach to music.

On that day in 1981 in the Frankston library, as I was navigating towards the hallowed ground of the Listening Room, the first thing that struck me (from about 10 metres away) was the distinctive (some might say garish) yellow colour of Emil's cover for *Computer World*. Even on a small cassette it seemed to stand out.

The next most distinctive feature was the caricature of the faces of what I took to be the members of the band, superimposed on an image of the Hazeltine 1500 VDU computer terminal, one of the first designed for home use.[6] They were rendered in the same garish yellow on a black

[6] The order of the band on the cover of the album – Florian, then Wolfgang, followed by Karl, and finally Ralf – is, in fact, the opposite of the order they would stand in their 'V' formation on stage during the *Computer World* tour.

Figure 4.3 Emil Schult study (Photo credit: Emil Schult).

background. The name of the band and the name of the album were written out in a very unusual and simple font.

There is no posed photo of the members of the band, only a track list and some credits. Later I purchased the album on vinyl and hurried home to check for photos of the band.

Figure 4.4 Hazeltine 1500 computer terminal art piece (Photo credit: David Sanborn).

Again, I would be disappointed. But disappointment soon turned to intrigue. Rather than the traditional photo of band members which usually adorns the back of a record sleeve, four robots in the likeness of Kraftwerk can be seen standing behind a bank of what looks like heavy machinery with plugs coming out of the back. The machines take up two-thirds of the back cover, with the androids looking intently at their computer consoles. In their black ties, conservative 1960s haircuts, and collared shirts these androids look like scientists in a futuristic laboratory or a nuclear facility deep beneath the earth. The background wall is reminiscent of the spaceship piloted by Thomas Jerome Newton (played by

David Bowie) in the 1975 Nicolas Roeg film *The Man Who Fell to Earth*.

At this stage, I didn't know if they were a real band, a band whose music was made by robots or perhaps a lone musician in a studio pretending they were a band. There are two photos on the inside sleeve, colorized yellow, black, and white. The first shows the four robots from the back, looking stiff legged, bent over intently, studying the controls of their machines. Hang on, these four could actually be the humans. It's hard to tell.

Finally, we have the four robots playing various handheld devices, as they would on the *Computer World* tour. In the photo, robot Ralf and robot Wolfgang are offering their instruments as if to say: this is easy, I can do it, so can you.

As Wolfgang noted in his autobiography: 'The robots were entirely appropriate to *Computer World* – thematically, at any rate – because, after all, home computers are nothing more than electronic servants, carrying out our orders and commands at the touch of a button, and this is happening in every office, in every household and in every child's bedroom, day and night.'[7]

The liner notes, meanwhile, are a true representation of Kraftwerk's influences from Bauhaus to Fluxus; functionalism and didacticism as art. On the original pressing of *Computer World*, the liner notes read more like an instruction manual for a piece of high-tech industrial machinery than the usual credits on a new album. Liner notes normally list the musicians, their instruments, credits for songwriting, the

[7] Flür 2000:156–157.

producer, engineer, and other studio personnel involved in production, engineering, and mixing, the studios used, and the management and legal teams as well as record label personnel.

As with most things Kraftwerk, here the norm was not only ignored, but jettisoned completely. Instead, under the heading KLING KLANG PRODUCT 1981 DUSSELDORF GERMANY (which could very well be the brass plate on the side of a factory or on a piece of expensive manufacturing equipment), Kraftwerk list the personnel, or shall we say, 'music workers'[8] who contributed to the making of the record:

> KLING KLANG PRODUCT 1981 DUSSELDORF GERMANY * HARDWARE: MATTEN & WIECHERS BONN – PETER BOLLIG – MR. LAB & FRIEND CHIP BERLIN – HERMANN POERTNER – GERD ROTHE * SOFTWARE: GUENTER FROEHLING – EMIL SCHULT – PIT FRANKE – KARL KELFISCH – COMPUTERGRAPHICS SYSTEM BERND GERICKE ERLANGEN – FALK KUEBLER – MARTIN TEWIS – CAROL MARTIN – TAKESHI SHIKURA – IAN FLOOKS – MARVIN KATZ – MAXIME SCHMITT – RALF HÜTTER – KARL BARTOS – WOLFGANG FLÜR – FLORIAN SCHEIDER * KLING KLANG STUDIO: JOACHIM DEHMANN – GUENTER SPACHTHOLZ *

[8] Aikin 1982:4.

Under the category Hardware, we have Matten & Weichers, the manufacturers who created the Synthanorma sequencer for the band. Peter Bollig, Kraftwerk's instrument inventor/boffin/mad scientist is named next, followed by the curious Mr. Lab & Friend Chip. A mysterious musical duo perhaps? No, in fact, it was a rare rhythm machine and sequence controller produced by the Berlin based Friend Chip Company, who clearly had the same sense of humour as Florian. Also in the hardware category were Hermann Pörtner from Texas Instruments, who supplied the famous Speak & Spell toy used on the title track, and Gerd Rothe from the Düsseldorf division of IBM, whom Florian had consulted.

Next up, the category Software which, in the case of *Computer World*, refers to the graphics and font associated with the cover. Günter Fröhling, a photographer and film-maker who shot the 'Trans-Europe Express' promotional film, took the photos. Pit Franke was a student of Schult's who bonded with him over their mutual love of sport, and who illustrated the image of the four Kraftwerk heads that appear in the computer screen. Karl Kelfisch was also an illustrator who contributed to the cover. He had worked with the band previously, creating the graphic artwork on the cover of *The Man-Machine*.

Next up is Computergraphics System – the company responsible for delivering the retro Courier New font graphics used on the cover and the inner sleeve. Staff from the company included Bernd Gericke Erlangen and Falk Kuebler (a computer technician), Martin Tewis, and Carol Martin. Takeshi Shikura translated 'Pocket Calculator' into Japanese ('Dentaku').

We then move to more traditional credits with Ian Flooks, who was Kraftwerk's UK tour promoter, Marvin Katz, the band's New York-based lawyer, and Maxime Schmitt (Capitol Records' label manager at Pathé Marconi EMI) who was a huge promoter of Kraftwerk in France, and had helped them have a massive hit with *Radio-Activity* (shifting over 100,000 units).

At the end of this list of credits, we finally arrive at the names of the actual members of the band. Ralf Hütter/Karl Bartos/Wolfgang Flür/Florian Schneider. No instruments are designated; no writing credits identified either.

And then we conclude with the third category: Kling Klang Studio. Here we find acknowledgements for their two in-house technical staff: Joachim Dehmann (sound engineer) and Günter Spachtholz (video and lighting engineer). A stranger set of liner notes you will surely never find. But at the same time, it's completely appropriate conceptually and artistically.

The cover art and liner notes for *Computer World* marked a conceptual change, a new way of representing the band. For the first time, the band members themselves were not photographed for the album, only their robot dummy likenesses. From this point onwards, the band would never again be represented, on albums, in publicity or in interviews, with an image of their real selves.

The representation of the band through their album art had evolved from the boffin image on the back cover of *Ralf and Florian*, into the passengers riding in a VW, reflected in the rear view mirror on *Autobahn*, then the faux-Weimar picnic scene of the band members sitting formally at a table with mock smiles on the inner sleeve of *Trans-Europe Express*, and finally to the cover of *The Man-Machine*, where the band are arrayed in stylized poses as though they are students of Walter Gropius, about to enter his lecture on 'Architecture for the Search for Knowledge'.

The cover and the liner notes of *Computer World* stylistically and literally erased the human. The band members were represented as being either subsumed into the new technology of computers (front cover) or transformed into Rotwang's 'Robota' from Metropolis (back cover, inner sleeve). The liner notes themselves were an artistic form of dehumanisation. The text is functional, sparse, and didactic, with a Bauhaus form-and-function mindset, like a set of instructions written for a new computer, or a set of operational commands for the Kraftwerk robots.

An instruction manual for the new computer world . . .

Before we examine the album in more depth, it is important to look back at its birthplace, not just a studio, but an embodiment of Kraftwerk's conceptual frameworks, frameworks that they brought to bear throughout their career, culminating in the *Computer World* album.

5
Folk Music of the Factories

'Kling Klang studio, that was our computer world.'
— *Ralf, 1982*

In addition to its themes of global consumerism, mobility and technological transition, *Computer World* is about work, the r/evolution of employment and the workplace in modern society. Kraftwerk's Kling Klang Studio was itself a physical manifestation and embodiment of these themes.

'Kraftwerk are like craftsmen,' David Bowie told *Rolling Stone* in 1987.[1] 'They've decided they're gonna make this particular wooden chair that they designed, and each one will be very beautifully made, but it will be the same chair.'[2]

[1] David Bowie was a big fan of the band, and while they didn't work or record together, they did hang out. Their relationship is immortalized both on 'Trans-Europe Express' ('From station to station, back to Dusseldorf City/ Meet Iggy Pop and David Bowie') and on David's classic album *'Heroes'* (1977) recorded in Berlin at the Hansa by the Wall studios. The instrumental track 'V2 Schneider' on Side 2 takes Florian's nickname within the band as its title.

[2] Buckley 2015:272.

Figure 5.1 Kling Klang Studio (Photo credit: Dreamstime).

For fans, the chair factory, Kling Klang studio, holds a near-mythic place in Kraftwerk lore, an unknowable and secretive location from which the most sublime and amazing music issued forth on an irregular basis. For Kraftwerk, Kling Klang was like another member of the band, an environmental presence that influenced the way they worked, and the music they produced. They also regarded it as an instrument: as Ralf said: 'we play the studio . . .'[3]

[3] Richardson 2009:3.

Following the demise of their first band, Organisation, in 1969[4], the Kraftwerk concept, although still just an idea shared by Ralf and Florian, was about to be fully realized. The pair were on the lookout for musicians, technicians, artists, and creatives who would fit their evolving musical template; they were experimenting and learning about musical composition, searching for their true sonic palette, their authentic synthetic voice, the appropriate vehicle for their conceptual obsessions.

When Ralf and Florian discovered the building in 1970, the 'studio' was just a disused room in an old workshop. Their first act in the creation of one of the most famous studios in music history was to fit sound isolation material into the 60-square-metre main room. Kling Klang Studio was situated on the outskirts of Düsseldorf in a 1950s building at Mintropstrasse 16, an industrial area close to the train station. Düsseldorf was known colloquially as the 'Office of the Ruhr', the industrial powerhouse of West Germany and of Europe, all glass, steel, and concrete. Quite a fitting location for the creation and 'manufacture' of what David Bowie termed Kraftwerk's 'folk music of the factories'.[5]

Bowie was spot on (as usual). The 'assembly line music'[6] delivered by the studio and its inhabitants was appropriately titled *industrielle Volksmusik* (industrial folk music) by the

[4] Organisation were the short lived, free-form Krautrock outfit that featured Florian's echo-delayed flute and flights of Hammond organ fancy by Ralf. *Tone Float*, their only album, was produced by German production wunderkind, Conny Plank, in 1969.

[5] Bowden 2020.

[6] Schütte 2020:27.

band. The phrase brings with it implications of Kraftwerk's anti-rock/pan-European-musik philosophy, as well as evoking their idea of a regional sound of the *Ruhrgebiet* (the industrial heartland of Western Europe). The band framed it this way: 'since we were into noise anyway, and we kind of liked industrial production ... we had this vision of our music being like the voice of this industrial product'.[7]

One of the best examples of this conceptual transliteration of the noise of industry, the 'voice' of an industrial product, is the song[8] 'The Voice of Energy' from *Radio-Activity*. The track is based on the words of German scientist Werner Meyer-Eppler, who worked for Bell Labs in the United States and created the first Vocoder, a device used to encode and decode the human voice, later used as a musical instrument. Florian subsequently progressed this original work on the human voice, utilising the Vocoder extensively in Kraftwerk's music. The Meyer-Eppler recording was known as 'The Voice of Power' and was used to test the newly created technology in 1950. The words he used were as follows:

'This is the Voice of Power.
I make it possible for you to have electric light and radio and television.
This is a giant generator speaking.
I am both your servant and your master.

[7] Albiez 2011a:23.

[8] 'Song' is probably the wrong word. 'The Voice of Energy' sounds more like a spooky spoken word piece recited by an ancient, broken-down mega-computer from the twenty-fifth century.

So, beware of how you use me.
This is the Genie of Power'.

Kraftwerk's 'The Voice of Energy' bears a very close resemblance to the words spoken by Meyer-Eppler in 'The Voice of Power'. Of significance for our analysis of Kraftwerk's conceptual focus is the retention of the key phrase ('I am both your servant and your master' (Meyer-Eppler version)/'I am your servant and lord at the same time' (Kraftwerk version).

All Kraftwerk's themes, from the robots of *The Man-Machine* right up to *Computer World*, with its new interactions between man and machine, are encapsulated within this one line. Incidentally, Kraftwerk subvert their theme in an interesting way on 'The Robots' from *The Man-Machine*. The word robot is derived from the Czech word '*robota*' and denotes 'work'/'labour' as well as 'drudgery'. The word was introduced in 1920 by the pioneering Czech playwright Karel Čapek (whose brother actually coined it) in his hit 1920 play, 'Rossum's Universal Robots.'[9] The robot as a worker, a slave, a 'demi-human being'[10] is an idea that Kraftwerk have played with throughout their career. The song 'The Robots' contains a phrase in Russian that translates as: 'I'm your slave, I'm your worker.' So, on 'The Robots', the machines are the servants, the slaves after all . . . Or as Rick Deckard put it in the film Blade Runner: 'Replicants are like any other machine. They're either a benefit or a hazard. If they're a benefit, it's not my problem.'

[9] Markel 2011.
[10] To quote the song 'The Man-Machine' from the album of the same name.

For Kraftwerk, the relationship people have with technology is not fixed. Rather, it is functional, contextual, and process-driven: the relationship changes depending on the utilitarian intent and purpose of the connection. The machines are not taking over. We are the creators of the machines. We operate the machines. Ipso facto (according to Kraftwerkian conceptual logic) the machines are us.

In the same way, the Kling Klang Studio is the embodiment of Kraftwerk itself, its nurturing womb, its place of birth, and like a mother, witness to, and generative of, their flourishing and growth: 'The studio was really born before the group' said Hütter. 'Everything came from the studio, as from a *Mutterschiff* (Mothership).'[11]

While the studio was not formally named until 1973, the phrase 'Kling Klang' brings with it implications of *industrielle Volksmusik*. Kraftwerk were interested in the sounds inherent to everyday life, that are often ignored or taken for granted, and are certainly not normally the subject or foundation for music. Named for the song on *Kraftwerk 2*, the word *kling* is the verb for 'sound', while *klang* is the noun for 'sound', rendering the meaning of the phrase as 'sounding sound'. Even in English, the clear onomatopoeia of the phrase denotes a mechanical, factory-like 'clang' sound. As Ralf explained: 'Sound sources are all around us, and we work with anything.'[12] In other words, the sound of everyday life, the sound of Kraftwerk.

Kling Klang was, therefore, never a mere music studio. For Kraftwerk, the idea from day one was to construct an

[11] Bussy 2005:12.

[12] Richardson 2009:3.

environment, a space in which to create and importantly, to *be* Kraftwerk. Much like Andy Warhol's Factory, Kraftwerk filled this empty warehouse with meaning; they would become Kraftwerk through making music, art, and exploring their ideas in this space.

In creating their music, Ralf used the phrase to 'put things together' in interviews very deliberately. Kling Klang looked like an industrial manufacturing facility from the outside and, like Warhol's Factory, where 'things' were put together, like a finely honed piece of industrial equipment, Kling Klang was the producer of Kraftwerk *produkt*.

In Warhol's case, the 'things' were people, art, music, happenings, film, and other media. In the case of Düsseldorf city and its surrounds, the 'things' were cars, fashion, architecture, heavy machinery, and fine art. And with Kraftwerk, the 'things' were music, cover art, conceptual ideas, video and film clips, and instruments. These 'things' were produced by the *musik-arbeiter* (the musical workers) of Kraftwerk – the management – Ralf, Florian, Wolfgang, and Karl, and their 'staff team' – Emil, Peter, Joachim, and Günter.

As always, the band stretched this concept to breaking point. In early interviews, Ralf and Florian expressed their relationship in the form of a mathematical formula:

E^2 (Kling + Klang) = 1xD.[13]

[13] Note: this is my interpretation of the formula for the purposes of the book, based on an interview with Ralf and Florian in which they described themselves as Mr Kling and Mr Klang.

E² = [when you combine 2 x ***Einzelgänger*** (mavericks) together – Mr Kling (Ralf) and Mr Klang (Florian) – you produce 1 x ***Doppelgänger*** (Doppelganger, the German mythological 'evil twin' or look-alike)].[14]

That Kraftwerk wanted to move with the times of the emerging computer age is not surprising. Throughout their career the band have explored notions of movement and transition and their focus on the new era of computing was a progression and evolution of their existing interests and concerns. This theme is reflected in the lyrical focus, musical setting, and artistic framing of the group via their videos, record sleeves and approach to presenting themselves in live performance. As Ralf noted: 'Movement interests us, instead of a static or motionless situation. All the dynamism of industrial life, of modern life.'[15]

Kraftwerk have always been obsessed with travel. Movement was an integral part of their personal and artistic lives, as wealthy and educated Germans who were a train or car ride away from most of Europe. The band's preoccupation flowed from their philosophy that the world is not static, that society and the humans within it are in perpetual motion, just as electricity moves through cables, cars travel on roads, people move through the crowded streets of the world's mega-cities, the turbines turn and the windmills spin. As a result, Kraftwerk posed the question: If everyday life is in motion, and our music is an art form recreating this movement in electronic form, then why should our music

[14] Hasted 2020:6.
[15] Schütte 2020:101.

not move and change dynamically as well? As Ralf put it, music is a 'flowing art form'.[16]

All music, it can be argued, involves movement and change. Kraftwerk's particular point of difference, though, was the fact that the forms they sought to recreate and represent were the structured, repetitive, clockwork heartbeats of industry, the machines (cars, trains, robots, computers), rather than the organic and chaotic patterns and forms of society, people, nature, flora, and fauna.

The band used the idea of 'music as motion' as part of their project of distancing themselves from the cliched tropes of rock, which they characterized as a 'stable format'. Wanting to avoid that 'box', Kraftwerk described their electronic music as a 'very liquid situation', like mercury.

Not only do Kraftwerk document and elevate the mundane functional activity of taking a train ride or travelling on a bus, using a calculator, riding a bike, listening to the radio, or driving on the Autobahn, they take pleasure in its documentation. They revel and find glory in what others would consider mundane. In their research for the track 'Trans-Europe Express', Kraftwerk recorded various train sounds to use as guidance for the sound and rhythm they sought to capture. The classic song achieved the remarkable feat of reproducing the clattering sound of a train travelling at speed on its tracks while turning it into dance music, an amazing exercise in 'endless momentum'.[17]

[16] ibid:51.

[17] Pattie 2011:131.

Figure 5.2 Trans-Europe Express (Photo credit: Dreamstime).

Their music over the years has perfectly captured this movement from one place to another. It can be detected as early as 'Ruckzuck' from *Kraftwerk I*, through to *Autobahn* (cars and highways), *Radio-Activity* (radio waves, transmission of communications and radioactivity), *Trans-Europe Express* (trains), *The Man-Machine* (space), and the *Tour De France* EP (bicycles). In interviews, the group themselves have made much of their interest in travel across Europe and their engagement with the world at large, as well as their delight in modes of transport, being keen cyclists and trainspotters.

On *Computer World*, Kraftwerk stand in a world on the very brink of the fundamental, revolutionary, tectonic technological transformation of everyday life. It was a change wrought and engineered through human ingenuity; a combination of science, business and government, a change heralding good fortune and opportunity, as well as problems and difficulties. Kraftwerk were also moving beyond the German and European focus of their previous work, exploring a global phenomenon. *Computer World* is therefore an attempt to understand this burgeoning new world from the point of view of the consumer, who desires the products of technology, shown to them by 'The Model' from *The Man-Machine*, who is '... posing for consumer products now and then'.

Computer World also metamorphosed their usual obsession with movement and travel. In many ways, Kraftwerk have always used this concept as a metaphor for the idea of transition through time ('Europe Endless', 'Franz Schubert') and space (radio waves, satellites), from one physical (trains, cars, bicycles), emotional ('Neon Lights' 'Computer Love'), or existential ('The Voice of Energy') state of being to another. The record explores this dynamic at a global level – it is really a meditation on the democratisation and consumerisation of the products of technological transition as it is made available to the masses.

Computer World is all about the transition from the industrial age to the knowledge information age: from analogue to digital; from physical communication to electronic transmission; from paperwork to network; from copper wires to the ether; from mechanical to hard-wired; from real to virtual; from poles and wires to cables and satellites.

When *Computer World* was written and recorded, computer use had primarily been the provenance of government, the military, and academic institutions. This was changing though, and the record examines the impact of computer technology in the context of business, education, and for personal use in the home. The album covers a lot of ground in its exploration of this new world. 'Computer World' and 'Computer World, Pt.2' reflect on the possibilities of e-commerce, cybersecurity, and online espionage, while 'Pocket Calculator' imagines personal control in an online world and 'Numbers' outlines the implications of big data and the world of global finance. 'Computer Love' addresses loneliness, alienation, and online dating, while 'Home Computer' focuses on personal computing.

In addition to lyrics about the serious business of computers, Kraftwerk focus on some of the fun aspects of technological change as well, including the emergent arcade game culture of the late 1970s. 'It's More Fun to Compute' is a take on the advertising campaign used by the American manufacturer Williams for their pinball machines: 'It's More Fun to *Compete*'. As DJ Food points out too, there is a humanity within *Computer World:* even the titles of the songs such as 'Computer Love' and 'It's More Fun to Compute', 'suggest a way to preserve the humane amidst the galloping pace of modern technology'.[18]

The album is as much a warning as a celebration though, a cautionary tale. But far from offering a bleak dystopian nightmare, Kraftwerk use their trademark sardonic wit and dry black humour to save the album from being serious and straitlaced – a feature of their work since the early days. You just have to look at the back cover of the *Ralf & Florian*

[18] DJ Food 2013:1.

Figure 5.3 Emil Schult *Trans-Europe Express* painting (Photo credit: Emil Schult).

album, which features the pair grinning inanely at each other from behind electronic consoles covered in electrodes and wires. Or even better, check out Emil's masterful stylized Weimar Republic-era picnic setting composition for the inside cover of *Trans-Europe Express*.

The transition to a computer world had only just begun at the time the album was released, yet the band had done their homework. Emil had spent time working at NASA's Jet Propulsion Laboratory in Pasadena, while Florian had visited the IBM research facility in Düsseldorf to gain more insight into the newly emerging technology. This research was useful in informing the lyrics and concept of *Computer World* and came in handy a few years later when the band upgraded the Kling Klang studio and all the instruments and equipment therein from analogue to digital. Kraftwerk's concept of their studio and themselves as musical and artistic 'workers' in an integrated production system put them in an ideal place to address the theme of the emerging computer age.

Computer World represents a shift of focus for Kraftwerk from physical travel to the theme of personal mobility enabled by the technological transition from the analogue to the digital world. In the computer world, you can now use your new pocket calculator to work out your family budget, and your Speak & Spell toy will teach your child to speak English. Your Atari or Commodore 64 home computer will allow you to get rid of that old typewriter, type up a letter and print it out using your dot-matrix printer. Or you could use it as a gaming console, providing entertainment for all the family. Government security agencies and banks can keep better track of your personal information and finances, with all the implications (negative and positive) that entails.

The lyrics to *Computer World* indicate that Kraftwerk had certainly formulated their concept from the personal perspective of the consumer utilising this new mobile technology. Most songs are written from the first-person perspective:

'I'm the operator with my pocket calculator' ('Pocket Calculator').
'I call this number, call this number' ('Computer Love').
'I program my home computer' ('Home Computer').
'It's more fun to compute' ('It's More Fun to Compute').

As musician Thomas Dolby reflected, at the time *Computer World* was released, 'computers seemed too insignificant to be worthy of having an album title devoted to them. It was actually ten years before pop culture was really impacted by computers and the internet, yet Kraftwerk were highly attuned to it'.[19] The computer world had arrived and was already in the process of changing people's lives. Kraftwerk, with their keen eye for the future emerging in the present, were one of the first bands to notice and write songs about it, bringing these new possibilities into the world of popular culture.

[19] Buckley 2015:170.

6
Speak & Spell

'We live in a computer world, so we are making a song about it.'
— *Ralf Hütter, 1981*

'Computer World' is the opening track on *Computer World* and its companion piece, 'Computer World, Pt.2' closes Side 1. The track carries in its DNA the full concept of *Computer World*: it introduces the themes of white-collar work, the cogwheels of capitalism in the form of business and industry, everyday use of technology, and life in the modern world. Musically, 'Computer World' also introduces the complex rhythmic syncopation, with the interplay of short melodic refrains layered over the top, that is a hallmark of the record, and the core of the innovation introduced to Kraftwerk's classic sound.

At the time of release, computers for home use as well as for small business were making their way into the consumer market for the first time. The Sinclair ZX81 computer, manufactured by Timex Corporation in Scotland, was made available for sale in the UK on 5 March 1981, two months before the release of the *Computer World* album.[1] Designed as a low-cost home computer for the domestic market, the ZX81 used only four silicon chips and had a memory capacity of just 1 KB.

On 12 August 1981, IBM launched their first-generation IBM Personal Computer, the 5150. Expensive in comparison to the Sinclair, it was nonetheless a hit upon release. Acorn Computers released the budget-priced BBC Micro in the UK on 1 December 1981, but it was the famous Commodore 64 (or C64), an 8-bit model with 64 KB of RAM, released on 7 January 1982 at half the price of the IBM, that truly kicked off the home computer revolution. Apple released their first Macintosh on 24 January 1984. Kraftwerk did not so much predict a computer world future, as document the dawning of the Information Age and the revolution of home computers as it was actually taking place.

'Computer World' begins with a synth bass drum and a synthetic snare based on a high-resonating filter sweep.[2] A distinctive hi-hat loop is also introduced, followed by a repetitive two-note bass pattern which falls on the downbeat of the bar, and the second quaver of beat two.[3] The interplay of all these elements with the various melody lines delivered by the synths, particularly the syncopation of the '... third

[1] *Computer World* was released on 10 May 1981.

[2] A filter sweep is a short wash of white noise that exhibits a doppler shift in frequency. It is a now-standard technique used by electronic musicians to add pace and tension between transitions.

[3] Adam Rudegeair, interview.

beat that results from this operates as the central rhythmic element of the whole album' as Brocker noted.[4]

To the listener, this driving syncopation sounds a little like disco. It's funky but at the same time mechanical, as though you are listening to the music that a sentient computer had composed for its own virtual discotheque. The beats have a treated softness to them though; this is by no means a punishing sound. It is made even warmer by the sweet synth line that washes over the beats after sixteen bars, ushering in the main melody of this most beautiful of songs. The feeling is one of a door being opened to a sophisticated and chic nightclub: the music is pumping, the crowd is joyous, you seem to know everyone in the room . . . high fives and nods as you and your friends are guided by the manager to the exclusive VIP section of the club. You are one with the crowd, the music, the atmosphere. It's intimate, yet elegiac. That is the feeling you get when listening to 'Computer World'.

In the opening verse, the words in the first two lines that Ralf delivers using the expressionist vocal technique of *Sprechgesang* (a style that wavers between singing and speaking) are 'Interpol', 'Deutsche Bank', 'FBI' and 'Scotland Yard'.[5] In just six words, Kraftwerk manage to outline themes that continue to dominate our lives today: security of

[4] Brocker 2011:111

[5] Interpol is the International Criminal Police Organisation, an institution that facilitates worldwide police co-operation. The FBI is the Federal Bureau of Investigation, the domestic intelligence and security service of the United States. Scotland Yard is the headquarters of the Metropolitan Police of the United Kingdom.

personal data; the relationship between government agencies and financial institutions; the centralized collection of personal data; use of personal information by financial institutions, government agencies and technology companies; surveillance culture; and the infringement of civil liberties. Or, as the composer Max Richter said in a podcast, the song is 'super subversive . . . If you listen to the lyrics, it's a critique of surveillance capitalism.'[6] As Ralf noted in 1981: 'Our whole society is computerized and each one of us is stored into some point of information by some company or organisation, all stored by numbers.'[7]

The German version of 'Computer World' makes these security concerns and connections even more explicit. Rather than repeat the opening lines of the first verse as in the English version, the German rendition adds the following line: '*Flensburg und das BKA/Haben uns're Daten da*' (Flensburg and the BKA – the Federal Criminal Police Office/Have our data there). In the second verse, this line is replaced by '*Finanzamt und das BKA/Haben uns're Daten da*' (Tax office and BKA/Have our data there).

Flensburg is a city in the North of Germany where the *Verkehrsamt* (Traffic Office) is located. It is here that car licence plates and registration data were kept, so, when fines were issued, they would come from Flensburg.

The BKA (the *Bundeskriminalamt*) is the Federal Criminal Police Office, based in the city of Wiesbaden in the west, and

[6] Richter 2021.

[7] Buckley 2015:166.

is the German equivalent of the FBI. Kraftwerk were concerned about the intrusion of the BKA into the lives of citizens, having experienced the passport controls the Office had put into place as they criss-crossed Europe on tour. As Ralf noted at the time: 'When you get into Germany . . . they place your passport into a machine connected to the *Bundeskriminalamt* [the BKA] in Wiesbaden so they can check whether you can enter or leave.'[8] The BKA had been in the press for mishandling information and for other controversies at the time Kraftwerk wrote the song.

There is another reason why the pre-chorus sections in 'Computer World' are so ground breaking. It is at this point that, in order to underline their argument about the transformative power of technology, Kraftwerk introduce a 'co-vocalist' with Ralf on the song. The new vocalist is, in fact, an educational machine, an iconic toy from the 1980s, released by Texas Instruments and designed to teach children how to . . . *Speak & Spell.*

From the early days of Kraftwerk, Florian was obsessed with speech and voice synthesis. As mentioned in Chapter 5, inspired by listening to a transmission of Meyer-Eppler's 'The Voice of Power' on the radio as a child, Florian worked with several companies over the years to advance Meyer-Eppler's work and create a vocal instrument that could be utilized in the world of music. *Ralf and Florian* introduced the Vocoder into Kraftwerk's music for the first time on 'Ananas Symphonie' (the lyrics are just the title of the track repeated). *Radio-Activity,* however, was the first Kraftwerk album where

[8] ibid:166.

Figure 6.1 Texas Instruments Speak & Spell (Photo credit: Arsh974).

Florian used speech synthesis extensively, using a Vocoder and a Votrax speech synthesizer.[9]

The Speak & Spell toy was first introduced to the world at the Consumer Electronics Show in Las Vegas in 1978. It was designed by Texas Instruments as a 'talking toy' that had an internal library of a few hundred frequently misspelled words. The toy could be prompted to 'say' a word, and the user would then attempt to spell it using a push-button keyboard with the letters appearing on a small screen. For correct answers, the user would receive verbal and visual praise. For an incorrect answer, the user would be offered words of encouragement. Retailing at $50, the Speak & Spell was a huge success, becoming a cultural icon in the process, even appearing in Steven Spielberg's classic film E.T. They were an early exemplar of personal handheld electronics.

For 'Computer World' and 'Computer World, Pt.2', Florian had the genius idea of utilising the Speak & Spell to speak-sing the pre-chorus sections of the songs by typing the lyrics into the toy, one at a time, and recording the electronic answers. Brilliant on a number of levels, this unique contribution to the sonic palette of the song had additional resonance conceptually as consumers were being propelled into this new computer world. At the same time, using children's toys as instruments also speaks to Kraftwerk's innate playfulness, humour, and joy

[9] On *Radio-Activity*, Florian used a Vocoder on 'The Voice of Energy', 'Radioland', 'Radio Stars' and 'Ohm Sweet Ohm' and a Votrax speech synthesizer on 'Uranium'.

in both discovering new ways of making music and sound, and subverting the notion of 'authenticity'.

Finally, to underline the shift to a consumer focus in the German version of the song, an additional verse was added with phrases centring on 'cash machines', 'video games', 'computers for business' and 'computers for your home'. The transition to the new consumer/computer world was now complete.

Musically, 'Computer World' begins with a synth bassline that has a fast bright delay; providing bounce, a galloping 'Bonanza'-like quality, while in between the notes there is a sonic deflection to add additional disorientation.[10] To keep the cowboy analogy alive, it could also be said that the sound of the 'zap', Kraftwerk's version of a snare, is very much like an electronic whip.

The song is warm, with the frequencies and sounds well separated, resulting in little sonic clashing. The vocals are mixed at the same level as the instruments, subsuming them, just one part of the whole. It is beautifully produced.

The song has a dreamlike flow as the separation between instruments is not hard-line; one element seeps smoothly into the next. This enables the band to mix and match the different sections of music without disrupting the momentum of the song or causing dissonance. The chords used during the chorus are emotional and evocative, redolent of driving late at night through the neon glow of a city (picture a scene from a film by Michael Mann such as Collateral or Heat, with a pulsating score by Tangerine Dream of course).

[10] Adam Rudegeair, interview.

So, how are we to interpret the apparent disconnection in the song between the beautiful, enveloping, warm sound of the music and the broader societal warnings in the lyrics about intrusion into the privacy of its citizens, enabled by new technologies? The answer lies in Kraftwerk's non-judgemental attitude to technology and the products of industry. Kraftwerk can see both sides, the good and the bad. They admire the utility and design of these objects. They also recognize the downside risk, the impact on individuals and society as a whole from the misuse of technology. As Ralf noted, 'it's about time technology was used in resistance, it shouldn't be shunned, reviled or glorified'.[11]

For Kraftwerk, the potential problems associated with the machines we make lie squarely at the feet of the humans operating them, not the machines themselves. In this equation, the music represents a eulogy to the beauty, efficacy, and efficiency of technology, while the lyrics spell out the warnings associated with mishandling its benefits.

'Computer World, Pt.2' segues directly out of the song 'Numbers', a delightful meshing of the propulsive rhythms of 'Numbers' with the counterpoint melodic motif from the fade-out of 'Computer World'. It could have probably been more correctly named 'Numbers, Pt 2/Computer World, Pt.2' as it is more a merger of both songs than a distinct piece on its own.

The segue Kraftwerk creates is seamless and remarkable, achieving the sort of turntablist transition that hip-hop DJs were starting to explore in the US at the same time. While the melody from 'Computer World' plays over the rhythmic beats

[11] Bohn 1981.

of 'Numbers', the counting numbers repeat themselves ad infinitum. By the end of the song, the counting has sped up to the point of total mishmash. The computer seems to be malfunctioning and the synthesized human 'voice' has become indecipherable, electronic gibberish. It is like a musical version of the falling rain of code in the film The Matrix.

The reprise of the 'Computer World' melody on 'Computer World, Pt.2' (a brave decision on an album that only has seven songs, running for a total of 34 mins 35 seconds) has a wistful, melancholic, heartache quality which completely softens and humanizes the harsh attack of 'Numbers'. What seems at first to be a battle between human and machine becomes a merger of both, to the satisfaction of neither party. The song ends on a note of chaos (the sped-up gibberish of the counting machine) and order (the return of the perfectly enunciated 'one', 'two' by the very obviously non-synthetic, human voice of Florian). The melodic melancholy of the music seems to be saying that no one wins in this particular battle, that we must find a way to coexist.

While musically and lyrically 'Computer World' works as a perfect balance between the benefits and disadvantages of technology, the descent into meaningless babble at the end of 'Computer World, Pt.2' serves as a musical warning of the potential downside of reliance on technology without thought for the potential consequences. 'Pocket Calculator', the next song on the album, could be interpreted as an attempt on the part of humans to reassert control over everyday objects in the Information Age, a mini-rebellion and statement of supremacy in this new technological domain.

7
By pressing down a special key . . .

'Pocket Calculator. . .was really anticipating some kind of mobility.'
— *Ralf Hütter, 2013*

The second track on *Computer World*, 'Pocket Calculator', is a pop song, Kraftwerk-style. The music bleeps and burps, whistles and yelps in a jerky rhythmic dance. Filled with strange noises, the song is a surprisingly driven, hypnotic and trance-like piece. The lyrics are didactic, simplistic, and descriptive, almost to the point of absurdity, their astounding lyrical economy giving greater depth and meaning to the words when studied more closely.

Describing in acute detail how to use a handheld calculator (relatively new at that point in time), Ralf narrates the song in the most comically overenunciated/underemoted, deadpan voice ever used on a Kraftwerk track. 'Pocket Calculator' is fun and seemingly shallow, with a lightness of touch that brings out the band's innate wry sense of humour. This is a song that smirks.

'Pocket Calculator' was released as a 7" single in the US in 1981 on lurid lime vinyl with a centre label in *Computer*

World yellow. The vinyl was housed in a heavy-duty, see-through polythene bag featuring the four Kraftwerk head images and a cheesy illustration of a hand pressing a button on a calculator. The artwork is a classic Kraftwerk move, a combination of the band's dry sarcastic wit and a didactic illustration of which Warhol would have been immensely proud. The band's name, along with the name of the single,

Figure 7.1 Pocket Calculator - single sleeve, front (Photo credit: Bruce Butler).

Figure 7.2 Pocket Calculator - single sleeve, back (Photo credit: Bruce Butler).

can be seen in English, in the *Computer World* album cover font, vertically orientated, on the front of the bag. On the B-side, Kraftwerk included a Japanese version of the song ('Dentaku' or 電), with Japanese characters used on the flipside to denote the band and the name of the song. This single is still very collectable today. The aesthetic effect of using the Japanese hiragana syllabary on the sleeve is to further connect the music to the imputed technological expertise and knowledge that has characterized global perspectives on Japan as a high-tech nation since the 1960s.

The single was recorded in other languages as well. The German edition of the *Computer World* album included German lyrics ('Taschenrechner'); similarly, the French release featured Ralf narrating the lyrics in French ('Mini Calculateur'). Finally, an Italian version of the song has also been played live by the band on a number of occasions ('Mini Calcolatore').

The idea behind recording the song in multiple languages was both savvy marketing – alternative-language versions giving the song a potential sales boost in markets such as France where the band had an established fan base – and conceptually in tune with the global lens of the record.

Like 'Computer World' and 'Computer World, Pt.2', the 'instruments' used on 'Pocket Calculator' were interesting, unusual and, in some cases, jerry-built inventions. Typically, it was Florian, with help from Peter Bollig and Wolfgang, who drove these technological innovations and advances. The instruments utilized on 'Pocket Calculator' include a Bee Gees Rhythm Machine, a Casio FX-501P programmable calculator, a Stylophone, and a homemade mini percussion device.

The Bee Gees Rhythm Machine was a small, handheld electronic musical toy with a keyboard, manufactured by Mattel and released in 1978 to cash in on the success of Saturday Night Fever and the amazing Bee Gees soundtrack to the film. The keyboard had 20 keys (A to E) with four blue buttons at the top. One button controlled the tempo while the other three simulated 'disco', 'Latin' and 'pop' rhythms. The toy also had a tuning knob and a volume knob, and the user could adjust the pitch one octave in both directions. The toy even came with a music book. Robot Ralf can be seen sporting the Bee Gees Rhythm Machine in a stylized pose on the inside cover of *Computer World.*

Manufactured by Casio in 1979, the FX-501P was a programmable algebraic logic calculator with 50 keys, featuring an early example of an LCD (liquid crystal display) screen. It features on the cover of the 'Pocket Calculator' single. Most appropriately, the screen had a yellow filter, a match for the cover of *Computer World.* The FX-501P was

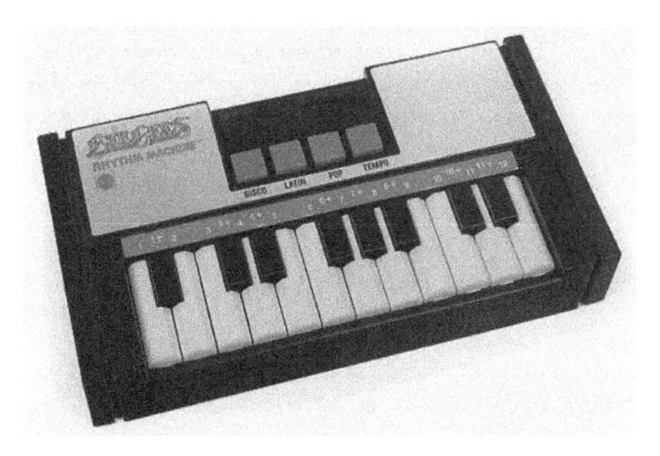

Figure 7.3 Bee Gees Rhythm Machine from Mattel Toys (Photo credit: Dreamstime).

the first calculator that could be programmed to play music by connecting it to an FA-1 interface manufactured for the purpose by Casio.

In a wonderful piece of marketing intuition, Kraftwerk asked Casio to manufacture a 'Kraftwerk' calculator. Based on the Casio VL-80 model, the 'Kraftwerk *Taschenrechner*' even came with a little instruction manual, a form of sheet music, showing the user how to play Kraftwerk songs such as 'Autobahn', 'Computer Love', 'Trans-Europe Express' and 'The Model', using the numbers on the calculator.
For 'Computer World', the instructions were as follows:

> 5203 5203 8536 5203 56 #6 #6 6452 56 #6 #6 645
> 56 #6 #6 6452 56 #6 #6 45

On the *Computer World* tour, Kraftwerk *Taschenrechners* were available for sale. These small handheld devices that were compact, utilitarian, but also capable, in Kraftwerk's hands at least, of creating art, aligned with their idea of the technology of the everyday. The idea of selling them at gigs was partly clever marketing and merchandising, while at the same time being arch commentary on the dividing line between art and commerce.

The Stylophone was a small electronic instrument featuring a mini keyboard printed on a metal strip. The instrument had only one sound, which could be keyed at different pitches using a metal pin on the end of a lead. The band found the Stylophone in a music shop in Düsseldorf. In a similar vein to the Bee Gees Rhythm Machine and the Speak & Spell, Stylophones were regarded as toys rather than

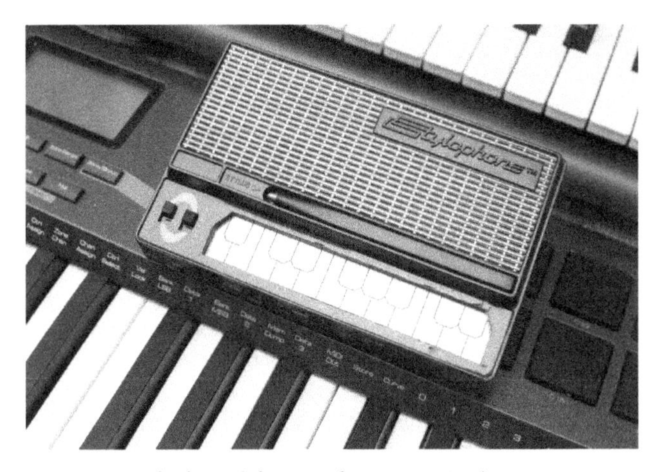

Figure 7.4 Stylophone (Photo credit: Dreamstime).

'authentic' instruments. Robot Karl can be seen playing the Stylophone on the inner sleeve of *Computer World*.

Finally, Robot Wolfgang seems to be hitting a metal box in the photo. The fourth 'everyday' instrument on 'Pocket Calculator' is homemade, as described by the real Wolfgang. He built a mini-drum pad using a flat aluminium lunchbox, onto which he screwed three rectangular metal plates. He insulated the plates from the metal case using plastic wrap. He then connected the three metal contact pads, each with their own assigned tone, to his console, which utilized Simmons SDS-V drum synthesizer modules via a long cable. Ha-Jo Wiechers, from Matten & Wiechers, created this console which had six 'triggers' (metal rods) called a *triggersumme* (trigger switch) to enable Wolfgang to activate the drum sounds.'[1]

Reminiscent of Devo's angular, deliberately self-conscious geek-techno-funk, 'Pocket Calculator' brings to mind a duck paddling across a lake. The song is deceptively simple and straightforward: calm and reassuring on top, while underneath, it is quite complex, with many musical moving parts.

The song has a very unusual structure. It begins with the chorus, then the verse. This sequence is repeated twice until the halfway mark of the song. At this point, the break arrives with the stanza beginning: 'By pressing down a special key. . .' The break is extended from this point until the last minute of the song, when finally, the chorus is repeated once and then a musical outro takes us into the next song ('Numbers'). 'Pocket Calculator' begins by establishing a consistent beat that features a gap on the back half of the bar, which creates a form of rhythmic hesitation. Kraftwerk fill this space with synth motifs, basslines and other tones. Each musical element is like an interlocking part that has its own 'musical pocket'. The renowned jazz musicologist Mark Levine defines a musical pocket as 'grooving, where the rhythm section is locked in and working as a unit . . . [where] the music is rhythmically in a groove'.[2] Within that pocket there is room for some improvisation, but the rhythm has a relatively fixed place in the bar even if the note changes slightly. Is this another arch Kraftwerkian joke? Are they ironically playing with the concept of 'pocket' in a song called 'Pocket Calculator'?

[1] Flür 2000:155.

[2] Levine 1995.

The band also throw in some musical elements that contribute an organic feel to the song. For example, the bleeps of the Speak & Spell samples are not quite in time but are purposely 'out', generating a feeling of disorientation, surrounded as they are by rhythmic regularity. This creates a woozy, dissonant, rhythmic effect akin to Thelonious Monk.[3] The middle sections of the song anticipate the arrival of techno and house music by several years, a clear antecedent to the forms of music that would soon dominate the dance floors and pop charts of the world over the next decade and more.

While the backbeat rhythm continues, the lead line emphasizes a flattened 7th, creating a tension that the listener's mind wants to resolve.[4] Through this section, two monophonic synths are competing, playing on the off-beat, and focusing on the flattened 7th, acting like rhythm guitars in a funk song ('Controversy' by Prince is a good example). An additional rhythmic synth is introduced ('tschh' 'tschh'), which adds to the momentum during this break. Despite all the elements involved, the song remains cohesive and interlocked.

The effect for the listener is of a disarmingly naive melody with a modest rhythmic backing, but this surface simplicity masks an underlying technical, yet harmonious, complexity – the musical equivalent of a Swiss watch, or the ROMY tetrahedral ring laser used to measure minuscule fluctuations in the Earth's rotational velocity and axis orientation from a small tubular bunker in rural Germany.

[3] Adam Rudegeair, interview.

[4] Adam Rudegeair, interview.

There has always been a subversive element to Kraftwerk's words, a sense that, lyrically, there is more going on here than meets the eye. The conceptual aim of *Computer World* was to highlight the societal changes being wrought by technology, which were apparent even this early in the Information Age, both good (new consumer devices, freedom) and bad (surveillance culture, control).

Kraftwerk were already aware of the downside, for the populace, of governments and corporations using technology to push the world closer to the dystopian visions of A Clockwork Orange and 1984 in service to their own impersonal, voracious needs. Ralf told the *New Musical Express* in 1981 that *Computer World* was seeking to recontextualize computers, taking them out of their role as mediators of control, and placing them in a creative framework that was unexpected at the time. In so doing, Kraftwerk were trying to 'normalize' technology, making it neither good nor bad, just a tool to be utilized. It was a typically idiosyncratic, neutral approach to thinking about technology at the time when perspectives were more polarized.

The first line of the song (repeated twice) highlights the notion of personal control on the part of the user: 'I'm the operator with my pocket calculator.' The German version of the lyric has a significant difference. It focuses on the members of Kraftwerk themselves as instrumentalists: '*Ich bin der Musikant mit Taschenrechner in der Hand*' ('I am the musician with a calculator in my hand.') This changes the focus of the German version from the agency of the consumer in the new Information age to a wryer Kraftwerkian observation on their use of the fruits of industry to power their music in a completely non-rock way.

The lines of the verse begin with a description of the basic functions of the calculator ('adding', 'subtracting') that the user can access, but then veers again towards consumer agency ('I'm controlling') while adding the intent of the German lyric in relation to Kraftwerk themselves ('And composing'). The lyrics of the break complete the transition of the song to the creation of music: 'By pressing down a special key/It plays a little melody.' As noted earlier, the group would make this a reality with the release of the Kraftwerk musical calculator (the VL-80) through their partnership with Casio.

There is an egalitarian intent behind the lyrics, the sense that the band are also letting fans know that they can also 'compose' using the pocket calculator, something that was underlined by the inclusion of instructions on how to play Kraftwerk's songs on the Casio VL-80. The instructions for playing 'Pocket Calculator' itself were:

4599 845887 4599 845887 6
4599 845887 4599 845887 6
44284 44284 44284 48244

Kraftwerk were presciently anticipating the revolution in home studio technology. Affordable home recording had begun in 1979 with the TASCAM Portastudio (a four-track recorder which utilized a standard audio cassette tape), and would be transformed by the new computer world, leading eventually to the plethora of laptop-based, professional digital audio workstation software such as ProTools and Cubase that are ubiquitous among recording artists today.

In the *Computer World* set list, 'Pocket Calculator' was the last song before the encore, giving the audience a light moment after the highlights of 'Trans-Europe Express' and 'Metal on Metal'. During the song's performance, Kraftwerk, forever working at more than one level, subvert the whole notion of rock'n'roll authenticity by bringing their collection of 'everyday' instruments (the Bee Gees Rhythm Machine, the Stylophone, the Casio calculator and the homemade 'lunchbox' drum pad) to the front of the stage. Each member would rock back and forth with robotic dance moves while playing their instruments, offering them to the outstretched hands of the audience members to have a play. Florian even managed to outdo Jimi Hendrix by reviving that most cliched of live 'rock' moves and playing his instrument (the calculator in this case) behind his back.

The true intent of the band in writing the song was laid bare in the live context: nothing less than seeking to highlight the agency of individuals despite the forces arrayed against them in the Information Age, and the destruction of cliched rock moves forever. Using a calculator as an 'instrument' in the live context is both subversive (in the context of rock and roll orthodoxy) and emblematic of the DIY philosophy of punk and post-punk. Kraftwerk were saying: anyone can do it, you don't even need expensive gear to make music. This chimed perfectly with the times and was inspirational to the embryonic electronic scene in the UK, and the growing new genres of hip-hop, electro and rap in the US. For such a 'simple' song, it turned out there was a hell of a lot going on . . .

8
Planet Rock

'The music is just like Detroit, a complete mistake. It's like George Clinton and Kraftwerk are stuck in an elevator with only a sequencer to keep them company.'
— *Derrick May, techno pioneer*

Have you ever heard the story of how four white German musicians from Düsseldorf who wore matching suits and ties, had conservative haircuts, and played only electronic instruments helped inspire hip-hop, techno, house, and synth pop? Well kids, gather round, because that is exactly what happened . . .

'Numbers', the third track on *Computer World*, is the most experimental, atonal, purely rhythmic of its tracks. A sample of its beat, along with a re-recorded snippet from 'Trans-Europe Express'/'Metal on Metal', formed the basis of legendary song 'Planet Rock', Afrika Bambaataa and the Soulsonic Force's early hip-hop masterpiece. Further down the line, the impact of Kraftwerk was still reverberating among the movers and shakers of hip-hop. In 2010, when Dr Dre, the producer who more than any other shaped 90s rap and pop, was asked what he was listening to, his answer was

'... right now it's Kraftwerk'. Kraftwerk's influence became an ongoing dialogue in music, incorporating other forms and genres. For example, check out jazz musician Jason Moran's version of 'Planet Rock' which features 'Trans-Europe Express' and 'Numbers' extensively.

It is little wonder this song captured the attention of so many forward-thinking pioneers; it features some of Kraftwerk's most arresting sonic innovations. The Karl-Beat, the Helix and the Electronic Sprinkler may sound like a sequel to The Line, the Cross and the Curve, Kate Bush's ill-fated first (and last) attempt to direct a movie, but it is, in fact, my attempt to label some of the idiosyncratic sonic elements that make 'Numbers' so interesting and unique.

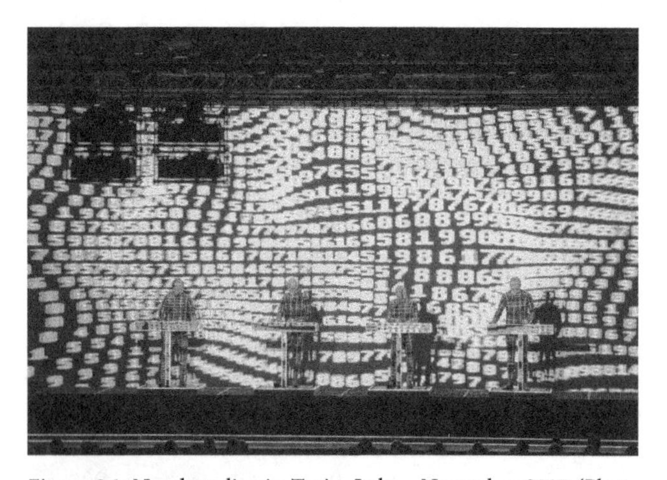

Figure 8.1 Numbers live in Turin, Italy – November 2017 (Photo credit: Dreamstime).

The track begins with a robotic voice counting briskly in German (repeated six times). After a few bars, three metallic 'strums' (up/down/up) can be heard, like a machine attempting to play an off-beat reggae rhythm on a metal guitar. At the same time, another German counting sequence is layered over the top, although at a faster tempo. You are immediately struck by the fact that these non-musical parts of the song are syncopated and rhythmically intertwined. This was innovative and unusual at the time of release, although through imitation and adoption by dance music creators over the years, the novelty has subtly become the norm in some genres such as techno. The voices are treated with a ring modulator to distort them, as well as space echo which generates syncopation as the dying waves of echo overlap with each other rhythmically.

Two ground-breaking musical elements are introduced 22 seconds into the song, which, for now, also signals the end of the counting sequence. The first element is the drumbeat, which was created by Karl (we shall call it the Karl-Beat from this point on). This is the drum beat that underpinned 'Planet Rock' and much of early hip-hop. It's a drum beat that sounds like no other, like an electrified lash hitting a metal pole at speed and causing a spark. It sounds like Karl tried to replicate an electronic hi-hat and then treated it extensively with delay and distortion, combined with a strange, abrasive, squashed-metal effect.

At the same time, a pitch-shifted sound traversing up and down the harmonic spectrum imposes itself on the senses of the listener. Free of the confines of a tonal centre, this sound travels up to a high peak and descends again in a frenzy of wobbling and oozing noise. We are hearing sonic relationships rather than notes per se – there isn't a chord followed by a tonic in this 'machine' music. It's a continual up-and-down movement for around one minute as the Karl-Beat and the Helix intertwine. There is no melody at this point either, just pure rhythm. All the instruments have delay and echo applied with a slightly random sync, which means that there is an overhang of sounds that layer up on top of each other cumulatively to create a startling and rich rhythmic effect.[1]

At 1:23 the numbers begin again: German counting to eight (repeated four times) and then English counting (to two). The counting sequences put an immediate end to the sound of the Helix, although the Karl-Beat continues with more echo and distortion piled on. Replacing the Helix is the astonishing sound of what Buckley termed an 'electronic bowl of Rice Krispies'[2] but which I will refer to as the Electronic Sprinkler.

The Electronic Sprinkler was created on the Minimoog and sounds like a high-pitched zap. Rather than selecting a sound with less irritant factor, Kraftwerk, ever the contrarians, instead decided to make it a central feature of the song. Short, sharp and repeated in quick syncopated bursts, the Electronic Sprinkler is redolent of the noise made when a fuse shorts, a high frequency that just cannot be ignored. It dominates proceedings for around a minute, whereupon new counting sequences are introduced in French (counting to three),

[1] Adam Rudegeair, interview.
[2] Buckley 2015:167.

Spanish (to three), and Italian (to four). With 25 seconds to go, Japanese (counting to four) and Russian (to three) join in on the fun.

Throughout this sequence, Kraftwerk construct the music in such a way as to lay bare all the sonic elements, spatializing the sound through panning the mix, fixing the Japanese counting in one speaker while the Electronic Sprinkler is emphasized in the other. At the same time, a synth filter set up with random modulation can be heard running through a very fast sweep while being applied to the Karl Beat. It is the sound of the robot owl from Blade Runner flying across a swamp at midnight calling out 'woot woot' forlornly with its mechanical vocal cords. As an analogue process, the sweep is not matched to the tempo so, wonderfully, it sounds a little different each time. This gives the song an ironic random, organic, almost-human feel; it is not as precise or relentless as you would expect upon first hearing it.

The effect of all this is one of disorientation and immersion. The listener is sonically plunged into a fully immersive yet unfamiliar sound world that could, for all intents and purposes, be Kraftwerk's recreation of the way an AI or computer might listen to music if it were sentient and could play back its own compositions. The sense of the 'ghost in the machine', of intention and agency on the part of the conscious mechanism, is foregrounded by the slightly out-of-sync filter sweep and the random modulation of the Electronic Sprinkler. Precise yet not perfect.

'Numbers' then bleeds into 'Computer World, Pt.2', with the Karl Beat and the Electronic Sprinkler continuing on (as well as counting in German and English) while the synth melody from 'Computer World' washes over the top. It's not so much a segue as a melding and morphing of one song within another.

In the final minute of 'Computer World, Pt.2', as previously noted, the counting speeds up to such an extent that it becomes unintelligible gibberish. In the final 30 seconds, we hear very clear and distinct German, English while, eventually, Italian counting begins again over the top of the high-speed yammering. 'Numbers' doesn't so much end, as take over a remnant of a previous song like an unstoppable virus seeking to dominate host cells.

There is a sense that the warmth and sunlit melodic glide of 'Computer World' has been brought back by the band in order to interact and do battle with the 'alien' sound force that is 'Numbers', a clash between light and dark, human and non-human. From the sound of it, the sentient world comes off second-best in this skirmish.

As with the previous two songs on the album, 'Numbers' introduces a new 'instrument': an everyday item from the emerging world of electronic consumer goods, the Texas Instruments Language Translator. The translator looked like a very large calculator and was used to count out all the number sequences in the seven languages utilized on the song: German, English, French, Spanish, Italian, Japanese and Russian. The translator was both the lead 'vocalist' on the track and an instrument yet, in the real world, it was neither.

Released in 1979, the Language Translator was technically similar to the Speak & Spell and featured two innovative

Figure 8.2 Texas Instruments Language Translator (Photo credit: Classic Cadillac).

micro-chips: a TMC0270 single-chip micro-controller and a TMS5110 Voice Synthesis Processor (VSP). With a yellow fluorescent display, the base model incorporated four languages – English, French, German, and Spanish – but Texas Instruments also created add-on modules in Italian, Russian, Chinese and Japanese. The translator stored 360 individual words and 78 phrases that were 'spoken' by the unit and displayed. There were also an additional 239 individual words that were for display only.

In line with the album's focus on business, trade, computers and security, 'Numbers', with its use of multiple languages, more than any other song in Kraftwerk's back catalogue to that point, marked a literal shift in the perspective of previous albums, away from the continent of Europe and towards the rest of the world. This shift was a natural conceptual evolution for the band, driven by the wider prism from which Kraftwerk were viewing the world on this particular record. It was also reflective of the fact that their influence on global music was finally being felt in the rise of new music scenes and genres in the UK, the US and around the world.

This global outlook was also reflected in the album's production. During the making of *Computer World*, Ralf and Florian flew to New York to mix tracks from the album with the French DJ François Kevorkian. He was a massive Kraftwerk fan and had been playing their songs at clubs such as the Paradise Garage and Studio 54. A remixer, producer, label owner and all-round influential figure in New York dance music and hip-hop circles, Kevorkian told Ralf and Florian that their music was very popular with local black DJs and turntablists.

One of those DJs was Afrika Bambaataa, who had been DJing block parties in the South-East Bronx since the mid-1970s. With a varied and eclectic style, 'Bam' sought out unusual records by the likes of Yellow Magic Orchestra, Gary Numan and . . . Kraftwerk.

Unbeknownst to Kevorkian, Ralf and Florian had already had an inkling of the impact they were starting to have in the discos and the underground scene. In New York in 1977, they'd gone out clubbing after hours and heard 'Metal on Metal' playing. Astonishingly, though, rather than playing for 6.43, the song kept going and going, for 20 minutes. They realized that the DJ had two acetate pressings of

Trans-Europe Express and was live-mixing them. The DJ was Bambaataa.

At the same time Kevorkian was helping with the mix of *Computer World*, Arthur Baker, a New York producer and occasional DJ, was sought out by 'Bam' to produce his new record – 'Planet Rock'. Baker was a friend of Kevorkian and would often go down to one of his regular club nights to test out new material he had produced. One such famous occasion occurred when New Order recorded 'Confusion' with Baker and, in the song's promo clip, they can be seen dancing at the Paradise Garage with Kevorkian and Baker on the decks on the night they finished the record.

The final pieces of the 'Planet Rock' puzzle were John Robie, a talented musician who played synthesizer and keyboards, and John 'Jellybean' Benitez, who helped Baker edit the song using his quarter-inch tape machine. 'Jellybean' later found fame as a producer and co-writer with Madonna in the early stages of her career.

'Planet Rock' used elements (lyrics, melodic motifs, samples) from a range of songs in addition to the raps of 'Bam' and the Soulsonic Force. But it was Kraftwerk's music that lay at the very heart of the song. Their contribution gave the song, and the electro-funk genre overall, the space and rhythmic structure to allow the rapping to be at the forefront of the music, through the use of synths rather than the 'total' soundscape produced by a rock 'n' roll band.

The team recreated the Karl Beat from 'Numbers', which provided the core foundation and rhythmic consistency upon which everything else was layered. The Karl Beat on

'Planet Rock' should be familiar to anyone who has heard any hip-hop songs from the 1980s (LL Cool J is a good example). The second element from 'Numbers' used on 'Planet Rock' was the Japanese counting.

Finally, Robie re-recorded a version of the melodic motif from 'Trans-Europe Express' and 'Metal on Metal' which Simon Reynolds once described, in his own inimitable style, as 'a funky iron foundry that sounded like a Luigi Russolo Art of Noises mega mix for a futurist discotheque'.[3]

As a team, 'Bam', Baker and Robie created 'Planet Rock', a landmark recording acknowledged as one of the foundation records for hip-hop and electro, incorporating sampling, hip-hop beats, synths and rap in a sonic soup, inspiring artists to use elements, magpie-like, from across the musical spectrum. Baker described it as a 'marriage of electronic music with street culture and black music'. Kraftwerk's music was used without permission, although this was subsequently sorted out after some legal argy-bargy. At this early pioneering time, when sampling was in its infancy and copyright questions were yet to be asked or answered, borrowing sections of music was simply a creative exercise. The issue of sampling came to a head with De La Soul's classic album *3 Feet High and Rising*. Not all samples on the record had been cleared. Howard Kaylan and Mark Volman from the band The Turtles sued for copyright infringement for De La's use of a four-bar section from 'You

[3] Reynolds 1998:83.

Showed Me'. An out-of-court settlement was reached, as with 'Numbers'.

Kraftwerk weren't only there at the birth of hip-hop, either. The Midnight Funk Association was an eclectic radio show in Detroit. It was hugely influential on the black music scene and was presented by Charles Johnson, more colourfully known as the Electrifying Mojo. Mojo was a major promoter of Kraftwerk's music, playing 'The Robots' and 'Trans-Europe Express' regularly. When *Computer World* was released, Mojo played the album, in full, to his adoring audience.

As a result of Mojo's influence, several black and Hispanic musicians in Detroit started to form groups influenced by the Kraftwerk sound. Mad Mike Banks was the founder of the famous Detroit techno collective the Underground Resistance (or UR) who said he considered 'Numbers' the 'secret code of electronic funk'. The song was also central to the world of Jeff Mills, also from UR, who said that it sealed the deal for him in relation to techno. Carl Craig too was a lover of Kraftwerk, saying: 'They're so stiff, they're funky' (Reynolds 1998).

The godfathers of Detroit techno, Juan Atkins and Derrick May, created a DJ collective known as Deep Space, and tracks from *Computer World* featured heavily in their sets. But the signal moment in the development of techno came when Juan Atkins joined forces with Rik Davis to form Cybotron and released a song called 'Alleys of Your Mind' on Deep Space records in 1981. Acknowledged as the first techno track, 'Alleys' owed an obvious and direct debt to Kraftwerk.

It was the metallic, analogue rhythms, the Karl-Beat, that formed the basis for techno. Detroit was like a sister city to Düsseldorf on the other side of the world, both steel cities founded on manufacturing and industry, with vibrant and innovative music and club scenes. They both shared a fascination for rhythm. No wonder they joined hands. It was Kraftwerk's innovative approach to rhythm, the precise-yet-not-precise (so as to allow the 'funk') rigidity of the beat construction that provided the template for techno.

Kraftwerk were not, of course, the only pioneers of electronic music. At least as far back as Del Shannon's 'Runaway', Joe Meek's 'Telstar' (performed by the Tornados), the Beatles 'Strawberry Fields', and the Beach Boys 'Good Vibrations' in the 1960s, or Pink Floyd, Stevie Wonder, Roxy Music and Brian Eno, Hot Butter's 'Popcorn', Telex's 'Moskow Diskow' and Donna Summer's Giorgio Moroder-propelled hit 'I Feel Love' in the 1970s, electronics were being integrated into pop music to generate hits.

At the same time, electronic music was arriving in other musical genres outside pop and rock. Delia Derbyshire (co-creator of the Doctor Who theme) at the BBC Radiophonic Workshop, Wendy Carlos (collaborator of Robert Moog, who produced the biggest selling classical album of all time, the Moog sounds of *Switched-on Bach*, along with the soundtracks to A Clockwork Orange and Tron), Dan Lacksman's (of Telex fame) *Electronic System* albums and sonic experimentalists the Silver Apples and Suicide were all finding ways to break electronic boundaries. Of course, electronics were a key feature of some branches of the Krautrock family tree as well, including Tangerine Dream, Kluster/Cluster, early Popol Vuh and many other bands.

Kraftwerk were not working in a vacuum or pioneering electronic music on their own. However, in addition to hip-hop, rap, techno, and electro they most certainly influenced UK synthpop, both in sound and in its look.

The first synthpop band into the charts with a song influenced by Krafwerk were John Foxx and his outfit Ultravox! with 'Hiroshima Mon Amour' (1977). At the same time, a duo from Liverpool were working on their first single, 'Electricity', based on the melody from 'Radio-Activity'. As teenagers, Andy McCluskey and Paul Humphreys of Orchestral Manoeuvres in the Dark attended a Kraftwerk gig at the Liverpool Academy in 1975. They promptly threw away their guitars and bought their first DIY synth kit. Over in Sheffield, Philip Oakey, Martyn Ware, Ian Craig Marsh and Philip Adrian Wright of The Human League were plotting their career path on a Kraftwerkian diet of synths, primitive drum machines and sci-fi dystopian dreams.

These three bands, along with Daniel Miller's The Normal, laid the groundwork for Gary Numan to step through the door with a glacial, sci-fi fuelled image that mirrored Kraftwerk's robots, and a sound that took their melodic motifs to an epic and stadium-filling scale, and straight to No1. After this an avalanche of bands followed: Depeche Mode, Yazoo, Soft Cell, Spandau Ballet, Simple Minds, Heaven 17 (Ware and Marsh from Mk I of The Human League), Human League (Mk II), Erasure, and Bronski Beat to name but a few. Kraftwerk provided the template, and the eager young musicians of Britain took up the challenge. However, this phenomenon was not just anchored in the 1980s. One band's love of Kraftwerk resulted in the sounds of *Computer World* rocketing back into the UK's singles chart for the first time in more than 20 years.

9
Another Lonely Night . . .

'As the people here grow colder / I turn to my computer /
And spend my evenings with it / Like a friend . . .'
— *'Deeper Understanding' (1989) by Kate Bush*

The opening track on Side 2 of *Computer World* is the glorious 'Computer Love'. Alongside 'Neon Lights' from *The Man-Machine*, this song contains one of the most beautiful and wistful melodies ever composed by Kraftwerk.

'Computer Love' was the first single released from the album in the UK (in the US, 'Pocket Calculator' was the first single). It came out as a double A-side (45rpm single) in July 1981 backed by 'The Model' from *The Man-Machine*, and it reached No 36 in the UK charts. The single was reissued in December 1981, this time as a double A-side 12", again backed by 'The Model'. EMI evidently felt that a hit was needed to help break the band into the charts and that, however unlikely, reaching back to the previous album to uncover a potential 'sleeper' hit might be the answer. While it doesn't quite make sense today, in their heyday era of the 1960s and 1970s, record companies tried all sorts of tricks like this. RCA's hit-and-miss approach to releasing David

Bowie singles through the 1970s, where they would reach back three or four albums earlier for an A-side or B-side, is testimony to this mindset. In any case, the trick worked for this release, resulting in the song going to No 1 in the charts, aided by the video for 'The Model' and the subsequent airplay that engendered. Evidently, the pop charts and music lovers were finally ready for Kraftwerk's synthesized symphonies.

The melody of 'Computer Love' is striking in its simplicity, driven by a synth line of relentless quavers so memorable that, 25 years later, Coldplay used it to propel their song 'Talk' into the hit parade. At the time, the band were having a hard time completing their Brian Eno-produced album *X&Y* (2005), the follow up to the mega platinum *A Rush of Blood to the Head* (2002). Stuck for ideas and, being huge Kraftwerk fans, they wrote to Ralf and Florian requesting permission (in rudimentary German – clever thinking by lead singer Chris Martin) to use the key melody line from 'Computer Love' as the basis for their own song.

One version of the response from Kraftwerk (as relayed by bassist Guy Berryman) was that Ralf said: 'Yes, you can use it, and thank you very much for asking my permission, unlike that bastard Jay-Z.'

But I think this version of the story is better. According to Martin, Ralf sent a letter back to London with a simple and terse handwritten reply: 'Yes.' Computer says yes! Martin and the band went on to transplant the synth line from keyboards to guitar and proceeded to write the song 'Talk' around the bones of Kraftwerk's melody.

In addition to that wonderful, Satie-like eight-note melody, 'Computer Love' is driven by an unobtrusive synthesized bassline that rests on the softest bed of percussion. On most recordings in 1981, the electronic percussion sounds were abrasive, tinny, static and clashing. Perfect in the context of post-punk and new wave. But no one had achieved the sound that Kraftwerk delivered on 'Computer Love'. It is electronic, yet in some way cushioned. The percussion is sequenced and repetitive, it is the sound of a piston, moving in a continuous circuit, providing drive and propulsion. But the piston sounds as if it is far away, muffled, yet organic, as if immersed in some warm and safe environment. In fact, if in the future, humans were able to give birth to cyborgs (half-human/half-robot), this would be the sound of the post-human infant's heartbeat.

At the time, the first wave of affordable monophonic (least expensive) and polyphonic (most expensive) synthesizers such as the Prophet-5, the Arp Odyssey, and the Juno-6, as well as rudimentary drum machines such as the TR-808 became available to a generation of young musicians. But it was Kraftwerk who demonstrated, on songs such as 'Computer Love', that they continued to have absolute mastery over this domain.

As with many Kraftwerk songs, 'Computer Love' is not constructed in the traditional way – verse/chorus/(middle eight)/verse/chorus. The group tended to blend, dice, and chop all these structural elements together into an alchemical mix.

To understand this approach in action, it's best to document how the song unfolds over 7.19 glorious minutes. 'Computer Love' begins with the chorus, as introduced by a nine-note synth melody, presented solo. This is a disconcerting approach to pop song composition – the vocal and lyric would normally come first, followed by the riff (the nine-note synth melody). On 'Computer Love' this approach is reversed.

The iconic synthetic bass and piston percussion pattern commences (0.3 mins) and continues through to the end of the song. The pattern contains a subtle syncopation reminiscent of funk, using a semi-quaver syncopated grid from which random notes are deleted, generating a stop/start pattern which is herky-jerky and funky.

The 'funk' is also generated by using different drum sounds in the pattern. The basis of the pattern is a synthetic hi-hat sound supported by a 'snare drum' that sounds like an electronic 'thwap' and a kick drum that sounds like 'tchzzz' and only occurs on the 'AND' of 'four'. Together, these elements of additive rhythm bring the 'funk' to the song.

The instrumental pre-chorus begins (0:13) and then, after three bars, Ralf intones the words 'Computer Love' with a melancholic timbre to his voice to begin the chorus proper. When Ralf sings this line, there is also a hint of hope among the yearning, and this is underscored by a 'heavenly' major 7th chord. The interplay between Ralf and the music pre-empts the feelings of isolation, yearning and hope experienced by the protagonist of the song.

A treated piano solo, in a mournful minor key, interweaves with Ralf's chorus melody, as if participating in a duet. The line 'Another lonely night, lonely night' is framed as a sad dialogue between the lead solo synth and Ralf. All the chords of the song are firmly rooted in the diatonic triads of a G natural minor, which are made for delivering deep emotion. Kraftwerk's innovation on 'Computer Love' was to invoke an overwhelming feeling of the desire and longing experienced by the narrator, the lonely male protagonist.

Finally, the human is dispensed with (3:22), as the machines take over for an extended solo and instrumental play-out (we are not even halfway through the song at this point). Throughout this extended instrumental passage (4:22), slight variations to the main melodic themes occur, such as the synth solo. The sound is created using a 'string' patch, emulating a violin. This patch has a slow attack, fading in as if being played backwards on a tape-to-tape machine. The 'outro' section is the aural equivalent of Kraftwerk having a 'jam', within the strict parameters they have set themselves.

The gorgeous 'Neon Lights', from *The Man-Machine*, is constructed in a very similar way to 'Computer Love', driven by a pulsing, repetitive piano chord serving as the bass, a simple yet poignant synth line and a repetitive electronic pulse. The drumbeat is more rudimentary than the piston-like rhythm from 'Computer Love', but it does retain the characteristic soft, organic, warm feel.

While the aural backing is similar, the connections end there. 'Neon Lights' is Kraftwerk's romantic paean to nightlife in the urban city, with its 'shimmering neon lights' at the 'fall of night'. It is like a stroll through the streets of Vienna on a warm spring evening. 'Computer Love', on the other hand, while also constructed from a truly beautiful melody, is all melancholy and minor keys.

The protagonist from 'Neon Lights' could well be the same person featured in 'Computer Love'. He has obviously had a hard time of it, as if the song revisits him many years later to find a lonely, wistful, aimless man yearning for love, albeit on this particular night, a quick and brief version of it.

'Computer Love' begins with our protagonist staring at the television screen in his home (which he would certainly live in by himself) or possibly a hotel room. He is bored, pondering the possibility of another in a presumably long series of lonely nights. He is also at a total loss as to what to do.

At this point in the song, the listener is plunged into a universally recognized scenario. A single person, alone and isolated, bored, watching TV, not sure what to do on another (Saturday) night. The protagonist then latches onto one element of his loneliness: the desire for intimacy and closeness via a sexual encounter, fleeting and ephemeral as it may be: the need for a rendezvous.

The second verse brings the listener to the point where human emotions and love become mediated by technology, in which the machine guides interactions on an emotional, personal and, in this case, sexual level. This is a window into a future world of phone sex, online encounters and internet porn. 'I call this number, call this number/For a data date, data date.'

This line is repeated throughout the second verse, reflecting on current developments in 1981, while foreshadowing the computer world that we live in today. While Tinder did not exist back then, experimental computer dating services were certainly starting to make an appearance and these were the inspiration for the 'data date' in the song.

On 'Computer Love', Ralf's forlorn half-spoken/half-sung vocals are full of ennui and yearning, exhibiting a certain lost quality. Again, the vocals are mixed low in the sonic palette, simply another instrument, interwoven musically with the synth line that carries the melody. The synth is sinuous, sexy and beautiful and, while Ralf's vocals are melodic, they are delivered in a deadpan, sombre and downbeat voice. He sounds a little lost. In fact, the machine in the song, as represented by the piston beat supporting the gorgeous synth melody (as repurposed by Coldplay and many others), seems far more alive, organic and present than the human.

Kate Bush explored themes of love and technology in her song 'Deeper Understanding' (from *The Sensual World*, 1989) but in many ways, 'Computer Love' more closely mirrors the plot of Spike Jonze's prophetic film, Her (2013) in which Joaquin Phoenix's lonely character, Theodore Twombly, nurtures a relationship with Scarlett Johansson's 'Siri'-like virtual assistant, Samantha. Like Ralf, Theodore ends up unhappy, destined to repeat the same aimless patterns established prior to Samantha's intervention in his life.

While the male protagonist does move into some form of action by the end of the song by organising a rendezvous having called the number to book a 'data date', we are not privy to the outcome, as he lapses back into indecision and inactivity. There is no real resolution, and the use of repetitive phrasing mirrors the circular and patterned aural architecture of the song itself, underscoring the listless and aimless character at the heart of the song. We leave the sad protagonist behind, repeating his desire for a rendezvous and for 'computer love'.

In this way, 'Computer Love' aligns perfectly with classics from the Theatre of the Absurd such as Samuel Beckett's *Waiting for Godot* and Harold Pinter's *The Birthday Party*. Ralf's forlorn character is a dead ringer for Estragon or Stanley. Eternally fixed in indecision, repetition and stasis.

Why, then, is such a sad and sorry tale given such a beautiful and sensuous musical setting? In their darkly humorous, deadpan way, Kraftwerk are highlighting their theoretical speculation that, in the future transition and engagement between man and machine, humanity and technology, the machines are not necessarily the parties to be feared. Humanity is doing a pretty good job of messing things up all by itself.

10
Here's to the Crazy Ones[1]

'But if you don't like what they're going to do / You better not stop them 'cause they're coming through."
— *'What Time Is Love?' by The KLF*

When reading reviews of *Computer World*, 'Home Computer' is often overlooked in terms of analysis and focus. This is partly explained by the seeming simplicity of the music, which doesn't vary dramatically through the course of the song, save the innovative 'break', more on which later. Beyond the bright and shiny surfaces of the melody and driving beats, 'Home Computer' is actually an intricate and perfectly interlocking mechanism, a Swiss watch, engineered to perfection.

The second song on Side 2, 'Home Computer' is often described as a prototype for techno and house (along with the song that follows it on the album, 'It's More Fun to Compute'). 'Home Computer' was certainly influential, being one of Kraftwerk's most sampled tracks, including on celebrated releases such as The KLF's 'What Time is Love?

[1] Quote from Steve Jobs.

Live at Trancentral' (1990)[2] and LCD Soundsystem's 'Disco Infiltrator' (2005).[3]

Let's explore how Kraftwerk made the different elements of the song mesh to arrive at a sound that was so new and so influential.

Computer World is remarkably uniform in its sonic aesthetic, guided by a number of self-imposed rules, discernible only from a distance, once certain patterns and repetitions have been identified.

The music is constructed and composed with an architectural mindset. Each song on the album is made up of four or five discreet modular musical blocks or sections that are inserted, extracted, or moved within each particular track. In most cases, a singular beat, rhythm, or bassline travels through the duration of the song, tying the various modular blocks together.

On top of this foundation, complex interlocking beat patterns and syncopated rhythms swirl intricately, forming the girders, truss beams and stringers of the song. Voice and synths are layered over this base, interacting and intertwining, delivering organic, human moments (small playing mistakes that are left in the song purposely) or minutely improvised elements such as the shifting syncopation of certain rhythm patterns, that distinguish Kraftwerk from, say, straight

[2] A sample of 'Home Computer' carries the melody during the second rap break in the song.

[3] James Murphy (LCD Soundsystem) uses a sample of the vertical arpeggiated sound that occurs at 1.36 mins throughout 'Disco Infiltrator'.

Moroder disco productions (which are obviously brilliant in their own right).[4]

Lyrically, patterns can also be identified. Verse length and content reduce significantly as each side of the record progresses. The first song on both sides ('Computer World' on Side 1, and 'Computer Love' on Side 2) provide the conceptual and thematic underpinnings for the rest of the record. Lyrically, the final two songs on Side 1, 'Numbers' and 'Computer World Pt. 2', are minimalist masterpieces. Similarly, the final two songs on Side 2 are the Zen Masters of the lyrical world with 'Home Computer' featuring only two lines of lyrics and 'It's More Fun to Compute' reducing that count by 50 per cent.

'Home Computer' is particularly emblematic of Kraftwerk's composition process. It begins with a series of bleeps and blurps that would be familiar to anyone who has pressed the 'On' and '?' buttons on the Texas Instruments Speak & Spell toy. Which raises the question: was this an early example of sampling (another Kraftwerk innovation) or a clever synthetic copy of the original sound made by the toy?

The song is underpinned by an iconic bassline, created by Karl Bartos on a Korg PS-3100. The synth motif (which first kicks in at 0.14) utilizes a mode known as C-Phrygian (which is produced by playing the notes of an A♭ major scale, but with C as the starting point). Phrygian mode has a minor

[4] It could be argued that the very Moroder-like 'Spacelab' and 'Metropolis' from *The Man-Machine* are some of the only examples in Kraftwerk's music where an outside performer or producer had a notable musical influence on their sound.

tonality, with the addition of a flattened 2nd (in this case D♭) lending the sequence a distinctively exotic flavour.[5] Incongruously, it could be the soundtrack to Lawrence of Arabia riding a camel across the electronic game spaces of Tron (as soundtracked by Wendy Carlos).

The impact on the listener is disconcerting. On the one hand, the beats induce in the body an instant desire for motion and movement. Yet the Phrygian synth melody stimulates images in the mind of vast exotic vistas and landscapes. It's a juxtaposition that again speaks to Kraftwerk's desire to find a halfway point between the duality of Apollonian rationality and Dionysian bacchanalia or, in the lexicon of *Computer World*, between machine and man.

At the 30-second mark, a post-chorus 'weird' break starts, with a super-cool, slightly out, detuned D. The note directly contradicts the adjacent note played in the bassline, creating a huge clash. Analogue synths needed to be constantly tuned, something Kraftwerk struggled with during their gigs where the instruments became even more temperamental due to variations in temperature and the fact that they were being lugged around the world in instrument cases. In this case, Kraftwerk made a deliberate decision to encourage the clash, which they most probably happened upon during band improvisations.

Ralf's vocals do not begin until almost one minute into the song: 'I program my home computer/Beam myself into the future', sounding very clear and succinct in comparison to earlier songs such as 'Computer World'. As if to offset the

[5] Adam Rudegeair, interview.

arrival of the human, the song introduces a series of machine-like sound effects, sounding for all the world as if Morton Subotnick has been let loose in the Kling Klang studio and created some new noises for an episode of Blake's Seven. These effects were achieved by Florian manipulating the frequency shifter on the EMS Vocoder 5000. Similar effects could also be achieved using another of Florian's favourite toys, the Sennheiser VSM-201.

And then arrives a new signature Kraftwerk sound (the one sampled by James Murphy on 'Disco Infiltrator'), the vertical arpeggiator (1:36). Kraftwerk give this sound plenty of sonic space, allowing it to grab the listener's attention fully. The band layer in other instruments and beats to place a foundation under it. The syncopated rhythms become more regimented at this point while incorporating algorithmically generated pitches. Additionally, there is a call and response between the hi-hat *zaps* (a static, hissing *'tsshhh'*, *'tsshhhh'* sound) across the left and right channels. And then the return (2:21) of the vertical arpeggiator with more effects, reverb, and echo (courtesy of the Eventide Harmonizer) which creates a cavernous space to contain the music. This instrumental section is sustained for over a minute and serves as a perfect template for house music: rhythmic, repetitive, yet soulful and uplifting. And brilliant to dance to.

Kraftwerk introduce a new section into the music at this point, a sound reminiscent of windchimes made of glass, generated by a spring reverb chamber. This musical block contains even more space, as if the listener is situated in a cathedral. The echo is immense, and the delay applied takes seconds to decay. Meanwhile, off-beats keep the momentum going with the help of a pulsating ring modulator. It is all very organic, with the sound ebbing and flowing, modulating and changing. This section could be regarded as the basis for modern techno. It continues to build and build, becoming relentless as the song moves to the end. The beat stops and the song gradually fades on a massive wall of Eventide Harmonizer echo and delay.

Musically as 'Home Computer' passes the halfway mark, the song speaks less to the earlier theme of resistance and interplay between humans and technology (as exemplified by the interaction between 'Numbers' and 'Computer World, Pt.2' on the back half of Side 1); rather it appears that, metaphorically, technology is here to stay – the beat goes on, generated by the machine, for the pleasure of the human.

For an album noted for its economy of lyrics imbued with deep meaning, the lyrics of 'Home Computer' are near-to-throwaway (on the surface). What significance can we parse from the two lines on offer: 'I program my home computer/ Beam myself into the future?'

When personal computers first came out in the early 80s, users did indeed have to grapple with actual aspects of 'programming' through the use of basic programs such as MS DOS. This was a world in which word processing, OS 2, Microsoft Windows, and Office were far-distant concepts. To wrestle home computers into providing some utilitarian value required a basic form of programming skill and knowledge.

As for beaming into the future, the Kraftwerk conceptual programme was not about what was to come, but the present.

Even on their most futuristic album, *The Man-Machine*, the band focused on everyday utilitarian products of the industrial and post-industrial world, even if these objects were still at an early iteration of design and functionality in 1978. But the thematic and conceptual underpinnings of *The Man-Machine*, such as robots and cyborgs, were not really far-fetched or even future-orientated, even then. The use of robots in industrial settings had already begun and, while not fashioned into human form, so had the introduction of bionics, body-part replacements, transplants and other human body additions, augmentations and introductions in the medical sphere. As for 'Space Lab', it was named after an operational satellite.

'Metropolis' is a homage to the band's favourite film, and therefore a look back to the past, rather than a vision of the future. In fact, the most cyborgian moment in Kraftwerk's career is not on the *Man-Machine* album at all; rather, it is the creepy 'The Voice of Energy' on *Radio-Activity*.

So, why did Kraftwerk suddenly want to leap into the future? Using home computers was still very much a novelty in 1981, and the notion of using them in everyday life certainly induced a delirious feeling of the triumph of humans in remaking the world. The lyric reflects human ingenuity and the fulfilment of those retro notions of modernity to be found in the Bauhaus movement, Metropolis and the amazing objects Emil witnessed upon visiting the *Futurama II* exhibition in New York all those years ago.

Of course, these lines are also the very essence of Florian's sense of humour: dry, mordant and self-mocking. One gets the impression that he is satirising the future-fetish and the business pitch to consumers, the eternal promise of a better tomorrow through new technology.

The final song on *Computer World*, 'It's More Fun to Compute' is closely related to 'Home Computer'. While not quite as symbiotic a relationship as the final two tracks on Side 1, 'Numbers' and 'Computer World Pt. 2', 'Home Computer' and 'It's More Fun to Compute' share musical DNA.

To begin, they both use the same chord (A flat major). They are both lyrically minimal (two lines of lyric for 'Home Computer', one line for 'It's More Fun to Compute'). And, in relation to modular musical construction, 'Home Computer' has three sonic blocks, while 'It's More Fun to Compute' has only two.

As the music progresses on each side of the album, all the elements of the song (lyrics and composition) begin to simplify and become more streamlined. This process of devolution and synthesis in no way detracts from the songs. Rather, it is as if the approach to making music has been trialled and tested in the Kling Klang laboratory and, like a Bonsai master trimming a leaf here, a branch there, to create the perfect representation of a tree, is refined by the end of the album to the smallest, most perfect, constituent parts. No need for extraneous or superfluous elements in this mix.

This reductionist sonic aesthetic is a phenomenon that can also be traced to the final songs on the two previous albums: 'The Man-Machine' on the album of the same name, and 'Endless Endless' from *Trans-Europe Express*. Both songs repeat a single line in a melancholic reverie, closing their respective albums on a downbeat minor-keynote, as if fading away . . .

It is also worth commenting on Kraftwerk's sonic aesthetic here as we come to the end of our sonic and lyrical tour of *Computer World*. In reflecting on rock music, Brian Eno stated that it is 'built on distortion: on the idea that things are enriched, not degraded, by noise'.[6] Kraftwerk aimed to use noise as well, but they wanted to isolate it, give it space, clean it up, and give it a spotless foundation upon which it could be heard clearly, without having an impact on the other noises and sounds in the mix. This 'clean' sound can be heard most distinctly on *Computer World*.

The title of 'It's More Fun to Compute' is another example of Kraftwerk's arcane humour coming to the fore once again, in that the name is taken from a slogan emblazoned on the backboards of early analogue pinball machines from the 1950s: 'It's More Fun to *Compete*'. Harking back to the past to comment on the present and the future is a well-worn and familiar Kraftwerk tactic.

Ironically, given the implicit humour and the use of the word 'fun' in the title, the song is anything but. The feelings imparted by 'It's More Fun to Compute' bring to mind words such as insular, confined and claustrophobic.

In keeping with the structural refinement of the music at this point of the album, the song has only two primary sections. The first section, or sonic block, ending at 1:03, incorporates the chorus and the vocals. The second and final section is a completely new musical construction, an

[6] Eno 2020:196.

Figure 10.1 It's More Fun to Compete pinball backboard (Photo credit: Nancy Shoshinsky).

instrumental block that occupies 75 per cent of the song and takes the listener through to the end of the track (4:13).

The band employ sonic effects and sound in a way that creates peaks and troughs, build-up and resolution through a low rumbling noise (perfect for the dance floor). These peaks and troughs also create a hesitation in the sound mix which generates syncopation and the element of dance or funk in what, to the casual listener, may sound sterile or robotic.

At this point, we know that the jig is up. 'Home Computer' and 'It's More Fun to Compute' are Kraftwerk's equivalent of dancefloor stompers. These final two songs are about moving the body. Dionysus has indeed won out. A simple skidding drum pattern underneath provides momentum. The drum sound is very thin (most likely a tiny spike on the frequency spectrum) and localized, which allows the listener to hear all the elements in the sonic mix quite distinctly.

After four bars, the one-line vocal lyric ('It's more fun to compute') commences (0:15) parallel to the low rumble, and just prior to the two-note sound spike. It is heavily treated using the Sennheiser Vocoder VSM-201 and is repeated four times. The pattern returns to the opening four-bar instrumental with the addition of a shard-like front-end sound added to the low rumble.

Marking a clear connection between 'Home Computer' and 'It's More Fun to Compute', a gorgeous John Barry-in-James-Bond-mode synth melody is introduced, which uses the same C-minor Phrygian mode. The effect of the A♭ scale is to introduce an introspective, mordant and melancholic soundscape over the top of a jittery, fast-moving rhythmic foundation. This is the equivalent of the Lawrence of Arabia synth sound from 'Home Computer'.

Importantly, while all these different elements mesh flawlessly, Kraftwerk are composing as though they were Pointillist artists, painting minute dots on a large canvas. In this case, though, they are painting with sound, using all the notes in the chord but not all at once. As with Pointillism, all the dots are there but it is the listener's mind that puts it all together. For the listener though, subconsciously, the whole is an interlocking, flawlessly operating machine of sonic perfection. Just before the song finishes (4:06), all rhythms stop suddenly and the mournful end of the final synth note ends one second later, with a decaying delay that lasts for six more seconds.

'It's More Fun to Compute' is a minimalist dancefloor masterpiece, a suitably downbeat yet electronically funky sound to end the album on. As if to say: people of the music loving world, we have completed our work . . .

Kraftwerk had a habit of ending their albums with tracks that distilled the essence of the preceding song's musical innovations. Primarily instrumental (usually with one line of lyric), these tracks worked as a coda for the record, a distillation and epitaph, a marker that the work is done. In other words, a down-tempo chill-out track to end the night. This mirrored the literal process the band went through as they undertook their musical work at Kling Klang. At the end of each night of composition and creation, the band would retire for a glass of champagne and a boogie on the dancefloor of one of Dusseldorf's many nightclubs. Think of 'Endless Endless' from *Trans-Europe Express*, a mirror of the opening song 'Europe Endless'. Or 'The Man-Machine' from the album of the same name. But, unlike those records, 'It's More Fun to Compute' was not a winding down or coda; rather it signalled the onset of new forms of dance music and innovative sounds to come. Kraftwerk were passing the baton on to a new generation.

11
Neon Lights

'Just by looking around us – around our studio and outside – it made us see that we were surrounded by computers, that our whole society is computerised. . .'
— *Ralf Hütter, 1981*

While *Computer World* is acknowledged today as a significant contribution to twentieth-century music, contemporary reviews on the album's release were decidedly mixed. This is hardly unusual in the sense that music that is revolutionary and ground-breaking can be difficult to analyse with perspective and context on the first or second listen. A review of 'Pocket Calculator' in the *Smash Hits* singles column gave the band a back-handed compliment (calling them the 'forefathers of Visage') before wishing they had remained in semi-retirement.[1] In the same edition, David Hepworth gave the

[1] Visage were fantastic, a New Romantic synth-pop super group featuring Blitz Kids, Steve Strange and Rusty Egan, Ultravox members Midge Ure and Billy Currie, along with Barry Adamson, John McGeoch and Dave Formula from Magazine. Despite their brilliance, Visage were a short-lived group whose influence and longevity was no match for Kraftwerk.

album 4 out of 10, noting that while he was waiting for the next 'Great Leap Forward', Kraftwerk had instead delivered a 'bunch of non-songs about pocket calculators and computers that are ... predictable ... and irritatingly gimmicky'.[2]

In the 9 May 1981 edition of *Melody Maker*, Ian Pye was far more enthusiastic, recognising that the album was dance-orientated and therefore more accessible to the general listening public ('this is Kraftwerk's first pop album'). Pye summed up the album by noting that it represented a 'fresh direction within which they maintain their credibility'.[3]

Respected music journalist Andy Gill, writing in the *New Musical Express* on May 16 1981 was the most prescient and insightful in his reflections on the album when he opined that what set Kraftwerk apart from other electronic bands was the way 'they construct and combine several tunes and rhythms so as to leave space for any number of additional components which unconsciously pop into the listener's head'.[4] *Computer World* ended the year at No 2 on the respected *NME* Best Albums of the Year (Grace Jones was No 1 with the brilliant *Nightclubbing*), a poll of all writers on the music weekly, reflecting broad critical support for the album.

While critics took a little while to catch up with the album itself, Kraftwerk's world tour, the band's most successful to that point, would cement their reputation as a spectacular

[2] Hepworth 1981.
[3] Pye 1981.
[4] Gill, 1981.

live act and genuine must-see proposition, with word of mouth spreading around the world as the concerts garnered five-star reviews. When 'The Model'/'Computer Love' single went to No 1 in the UK charts in February 1982, Kraftwerk had completed their trajectory from avant-garde innovators to authentic chart-topping pop band with credibility and cache as electronic pioneers.

For the *Computer World* tour, Kraftwerk decided to take their workplace, the Kling Klang Studio itself, on the road with them . . . this was revolutionary. Reflecting the changing nature of work manifested on *Computer World*, Kraftwerk turned the idea of live performance itself on its head. Rather than an escape from the mundanity of a 9 to 5 workday through embarking on a world tour (the ultimate divorced-from-reality experience), Kraftwerk instead decided, as Pattie lucidly and convincingly argued, to 'make a performance out of their working environment . . .at a time when the working world was beginning to change.'[5]

The process of dismantling the studio and making it transportable, so it could be assembled and disassembled efficiently, was an engineering and logistics marvel. The recording of the album, combined with planning the tour, and having special rigs and cases custom built to cradle the equipment on stage and transport it to the next gig, partly explains the reason why there was such a long gap between the release of *The Man-Machine* and *Computer World*. This exercise was overseen by Joachim Dehmann (sound

[5] Pattie 2011:131.

engineer) and Günter Spachtholz (lighting/video) with input from Wolfgang and overseen on the road by Emil.[6]

The stage for the world tour was set up as an inverted 'V' shape, to enable the musicians to maintain eye contact with each other. In fact, Ralf said: 'The idea of the semi-circle was once again to portray the symmetry of the group as a working machine, where no one person or element dominated' (Bussey 2005:120).

Ralf stood on the far left, with Florian on the far right, each with a console that held their keyboards. Next to Ralf stood Karl with a drum console and a keyboard, next to him was Wolfgang with his electronic drum array. Out of sight, tracing the outer edge of the 'V', were the veins and arteries of Kling Klang itself, the cables and leads connected to the effects, delays, sequencers and other studio gadgetry. Behind the band were four state-of-the-art video displays, supplied by Sony, which ran films and animations created by Emil and Günter.

To enhance this idea of stage as workplace, the band presented themselves as besuited businessmen, workers, in full *The Man-Machine* outfits consisting of red shirts, black trousers and black ties. For Kraftwerk, playing the 'studio' on stage much like they played the studio back at home in Düsseldorf was an exciting idea. As Ralf proclaimed: '. . . we don't have Kraftwerk anymore, but Kraftwerk and Kling Klang together'.[7] Which raised the question that Bussy poses

[6] In addition to Emil, Joachim and Günter, the other two members of the in-house Kraftwerk support team were Peter Bollig (instrument technician/inventor/odd-job man) and Ha-Jo Wiechers (engineer) (Aikin 1982:5).
[7] Pattie 2011:129.

in his book: 'Was this a studio band playing live, or a live band playing the studio?'[8]

Finally, Kraftwerk and Kling Klang had become one.

One of the most remarkable concerts on the tour took place in my hometown of Melbourne on 20 September 1981, at an old, majestic 1,500 capacity theatre which opened in 1854. As Wolfgang remarked in his book: 'Our concert in Melbourne was scheduled to take place in the Princess Theatre the next day. We had no idea of the surprise that waited for us there.'[9]

Unbeknownst to the Kraftwerk fans taking their seats on that balmy and beautiful spring evening, there was some disquiet within the Kraftwerk camp. While this didn't impact on the entertainment that night, it was an indication of the inter-band tensions that would lead to the eventual breakup of the classic line up.

As per the usual routine on the *Computer World* tour; Ralf, Wolfgang, Karl, Emil and the other members of the band's entourage would go out for an early dinner following the soundcheck. Florian, as was his wont, would leave the rest of the band behind and go out in search of a local Indian restaurant, keeping to himself, and usually arriving for the gig just before curtain-up. With the concert about to start, however, Florian was nowhere to be found. Debating whether to cancel the gig or to try to go on without Florian, Emil, in a panic, looked out at the crowd through a hole in the curtain and spied Florian in the theatre, sitting among fans in the

[8] Bussy 2005:121.
[9] Flür 2000: 199.

back row. Florian didn't like touring, being forced to be away from the comforts of home, the nightclubs of Düsseldorf and the excitement of creation within the confines of the Kling Klang studio. He also felt that, over time, his importance within the band during concerts had lessened. Florian was eventually persuaded on stage to enable the gig to commence. Melbourne fans witnessed one of the best concerts of their lives, completely unaware of the drama, stress and ill-will circulating within the band.

The *Computer World* shows were spectacular. In addition to the amazing stage rig created to hold all the band's instruments, each song would be accompanied by visuals and films specifically made for the tour. Wolfgang thought they helped turn their stage into a 'shining control room in a spaceship'[10] while Ralf referred to the screens as part of his electronic living room, noting that '... we want the videos we show to enlarge our music, increase its prophetic and visionary side'.[11]

When the curtain swept back for the encore of 'The Robots', there were eight figures standing on stage; next to each band member was a corresponding, life-like 'robot' *doppelgänger*. A well-known Australian music industry personality I interviewed was invited backstage and noticed four long road cases on the ground. Upon closer inspection, he noticed that they contained the 'robots'. 'It was weird, they were like coffins that were ready to have the lids shut and packed into the back of the truck.'[12]

[10] ibid:156.
[11] ibid 161.
[12] Bruce Butler, interview.

Figure 11.1 Melbourne, 20 September 1981 (Photo credit: Bruce Butler).

Startlingly, the band did not break character after the show. 'After the guys took off their stage attire (red shirts, black pants, black ties), they emerged in black shirts, red pants, and red ties and pronounced that they wanted to go to the disco to dance.'[13]

After the gig, Emil and another member of the Kraftwerk entourage retired to the famous Melbourne Underground nightclub, drinking wine and dancing the night away. Quite a feat of stamina given that, earlier in the day, they had undertaken a massive bike ride, a soundcheck and performed a sell-out show.

[13] Bruce Butler, interview.

And so ends one of the most glorious and innovative albums ever released. Kraftwerk would go on to record and release more wonderful music: The *Tour de France* 12" (1983), *Electric Café* (1986), *The Mix* (1991), *Expo 2000* EP (1999), *Tour de France Soundtracks* (2003) and the live album, *Minimum Maximum* (2005). But after *Computer World*, the gaps between records were longer and their impact on other artists lessened as the drive to innovate and create new genres slowed down, as the weight of living up to their extraordinary musical legacy produced a paralysing, obsessive perfection that slowly ossified into inactivity.

Following the completion of the world tour in December 1981, the band moved its focus to transforming Kling Klang into a digital studio, recording a new album (originally titled *Techno Pop*, but released as *Electric Café*), re-recording a number of their old songs for *The Mix* and, of course, cycling. Gradually, the founder members of the band drifted away, lost interest and retired as a result of this long, drawn-out process (Emil in 1982, Wolfgang in 1987, Karl in 1990, and finally Florian in 2006). Karl expressed it this way: 'By the end of the Eighties, Kraftwerk were a paralysed giant.'[14]

This left the band in the more-than-capable hands of Ralf, who focused his energies on curating Kraftwerk's legacy through an ongoing series of live shows in the world's most prestigious galleries (V&A, The Tate Modern), music halls (Sydney Opera House) and festivals (The Tribal Gathering, the Latitude Festival, and the Manchester International

[14] Bussy 2005:171.

Figure 11.2 Computer World live in Turin, Italy (November 2017) (Photo credit: Dreamstime).

Festival, playing at the Manchester Velodrome). Using cutting-edge digital 3D displays, state-of-the-art sound systems and light shows, 'spectacular' and 'stunning' would be the best way to describe the modern Kraftwerk live experience.

Ralf would take up his classic position on the left side of the stage. The other three performers included a lighting tech, a sound engineer, and a rhythm specialist. Ralf was truly delivering on his philosophy of presenting the band as a group of non-descript 'workers'. He was the only recognisable musician on stage. And replacing the banks of equipment from the Kling Klang *Mutterschiff* were four lecterns, behind which Ralf and his barely moving cohorts

Figure 11.3 Kraftwerk perform Computer World at the Sydney Opera House (ticket and 3D glasses) (Photo credit: Steve Tupai Francis).

would 'play' their laptops, clad in (uncomfortably) skin-tight glowing neoprene outfits. Equal parts spectacular and discombobulating.

The true break with the classic line up occurred with the tragic death of co-founder Florian in 2020. But what a legacy they left behind. For a band that started in free-jazz experimentation in the art precincts and galleries of Düsseldorf, centre of nothing at all in the world of music, Kraftwerk ended up influencing whole musical genres, and in the process, becoming revered international treasures, something underlined by their induction into the Rock and Roll Hall of Fame.

Computer World holds a hallowed place among the greats of modern recorded music. Its influence continues to *kraft* (power) the *werk* (work) of creative artists around the world to this day. The band had completed their prime directive of musical revolution. Kraftwerk could now contemplate an easy retirement of occasional sold-out performances in the most prestigious concert halls on the planet, their legendary status confirmed, safe in the knowledge that from their Kling Klang studio 'mothership', four avant-garde artists from Düsseldorf had managed to turn their conceptual *gesamtkunstwerk* into a chart-topping musical enterprise, feted by critics and the press and adored by legions of fans across the world.

References

Aikin, J. (1982), 'Kraftwerk: Electronic Minstrels of the Global Village' *Keyboard*, March. Available at: https://books.google.com.au/books?id=IbtJAgAAQBAJ&pg=PT7&lpg=PT7&dq=aikin+keyboard+kraftwerk:+electronic+minstrels+of+the+global+village. Accessed 13 Feb 2021.

Albiez, S. (2011a), '*Autobahn* and Heimatklänge' in S. Albiez and D. Pattie (eds) *Kraftwerk: Music Non-Stop*. New York: The Continuum International Publishing Group.

Albiez, S. (2011b), 'Europe Non-Stop: West Germany, Britain and the Rise of Synthpop, 1975–81' in S. Albiez and D. Pattie (eds) *Kraftwerk: Music Non-Stop*. New York: The Continuum International Publishing Group.

Anderson, J. (2020), '02_Kraftwerk', in J. Robinson (ed.) *The Ultimate Music Guide: Kraftwerk*. London: Bandcamp Technologies.

Baudelaire, C. (1964) [1863], *The Painter of Modern Life and Other Essays*, (edited and translated by Jonathan Mayne). London: Phaidon Press.

Beecher, M. (1981), 'Kraftwerk Revealed: An Interview with Ralf Hütter' *Electronics and Music Maker*, September. Available at: www.muzines.co.uk/mags/emm/81/09/594. Accessed 6 April 2021.

Bohn, C. (1981), 'We have nobody to listen to . . .' *New Musical Express*, 13 June, 1981.

Bowden, M. (2020), 'The Elusive Florian Schneider' *New Directions in Music*, 2020. Available at: www.newdirectionsinmusic.com/the-elusive-florian-schneider/. Accessed 5 August 2021.

Brocker, C. (2011), 'Kraftwerk: Technology and Composition', in S. Albiez and D. Pattie (eds) *Kraftwerk: Music Non-Stop*. New York: The Continuum International Publishing Group.

Buckley, D. (2015), *Kraftwerk Pubikation: A Biography*. London: Omnibus Press.

Bussy, P. (2005), *Kraftwerk: Man, Machine and Music*. London: SAF Publishing.

Crowe, C. (1976), 'David Bowie: Ground Control to Davy Jones' *Rolling Stone*, 12 February.

Cunningham, D. (2011), 'Kraftwerk and the Image of the Modern', in S. Albiez and D. Pattie (eds) *Kraftwerk: Music Non-Stop*. New York: The Continuum International Publishing Group.

Dale, J. (2020), '04_Ralf and Florian', in J. Robinson (ed.) *The Ultimate Music Guide: Kraftwerk*. London: Bandcamp Technologies.

Dallas, K. (1975), 'We Are Not Part of the Musical World', *Melody Maker*. 27 September.

Eno, B. (2020 [1996]), *A Year with Swollen Appendices: Brian Eno's Diary*. London: Faber and Faber.

Ewing, T. (2009), 'Kraftwerk: The Catalogue'. Pitchfork, December. Available at: https://pitchfork.com/reviews/albums/13742-the-catalogue/. Accessed 29 June 2020.

Flür, W. (2000), *Kraftwerk: I Was a Robot*. London: Sanctuary Publishing.

Food, D.J. (2013), 'Kraftwerk: Computer World'. Clashmusic. 2 November. Available at: www.clashmusic.com/features/kraftwerk-computer-world. Accessed 29 June 2020.

Gill, A. (1981), 'Kraftwerk: Computer World'. *New Musical Express*. 16 May. London.

Harraway, D. (1985), 'A cyborg manifesto' in S. During (ed.) *The Cultural Studies Reader*. London: Routledge.

Hasted, N. (2020), '01_Tone Float', in J. Robinson (ed) *The Ultimate Music Guide: Kraftwerk*. London: Bandcamp Technologies.

Hayles, N.K. (1999), *How We Became Posthuman*, Chicago: University of Chicago Press.

Hepworth, D. (1981), 'Kraftwerk's Computer World'. *Smash Hits*, 12 May. London.

Hütter, R. (2013), 'Kraftwerk – Album by Album'. *Uncut*, 4 January. London.

Jonze, T. (2017), 'Kraftwerk's Ralf Hütter: 'Music is about intensity . . . the rest is just noise'. *The Guardian*, 16 June. Available at: www.theguardian.com/music/2017/jun/15/kraftwerk-ralf-hutter-music-about-intensity-the-rest-is-just-noise. Accessed 10 July 2021.

Levine, M. (1995), *The Jazz Theory Book*, London: Sher Music Co.

Locke, J. (2020), 'Remembering Kraftwerk's Florian Schneider Through His Most Widely Overlooked Work'. Flood Magazine, 8May. Available at: https://floodmagazine.com/77696/rem8 embering-kraftwerks-florian-schneider-through-his-most-widely-overlooked-work/ Accessed 4 June, 2021.

Lynskey, D. (2014), 'Kraftwerk at Tate Modern, Night Five: Computer World'. *The Guardian*, 13 February. Available at: www.theguardian.com/music/musicblog/2013/feb/12/kraftwerk-tate-modern-five-computer-world. Accessed 11 April, 2021.

Markel, H. (2011), 'The Origin of the Word 'Robot''. Science Friday, 22 April. Available at: www.sciencefriday.com/segments/the-origin-of-the-word-robot/. Accessed 1 August, 2021.

Meyer-Eppler, W. (1950), 'The Voice of Power'. Available at: https://archive.org/details/meyer-eppler-werner-the-voice-of-power. Accessed 4 April, 2021.

Norman, D. (1988), *The Design of Everyday Things*. New York: Basic Books.

Passmore, G. and Proesch, G. (1970), 'The Laws of Sculptors (1969)'. *Studio International*. May 1970.

Pattie, D. (2011), 'Kraftwerk: Playing the Machines', in S. Albiez and D. Pattie (eds) *Kraftwerk: Music Non-Stop*. New York: The Continuum International Publishing Group.

Pattison, L. (2020), '06_Radio-Activity', in J. Robinson (ed) *The Ultimate Music Guide: Kraftwerk*. London: Bandcamp Technologies.

Power, C. (2009), 'Computer World: Remastered'. Drowned in Sound, 14 October. Available at: https://drownedinsound.com/releases/14742/reviews/4138139 accessed 8 December 2020.

Pye, I. (1981), 'Computer World review'. *Melody Maker*, 9 May. London.

Reid, G. (2008), '*Interview:*Ralf Hütter of Kraftwerk'. NZ Herald, 27 September. Available at: www.nzherald.co.nz/entertainment/iinterviewi-ralf-hutter-of-kraftwerk/ODY2FSVHWCJFE23ZJZ4AEEL6NY/. Accessed 10 July 2021.

Reitveld, H. (2011), 'Trans-Europa Express: Tracing the Trance Machine', in S. Albiez and D. Pattie (eds) *Kraftwerk: Music Non-Stop*. New York: The Continuum International Publishing Group.

Reynolds, S. (1998), *Energy Flash: A Journey Through Rave Music and Dance Culture*, London: Faber and Faber.

Richardson, M. (2009), 'Interview with Ralf Hütter from Kraftwerk'. Pitchfork, November. Available at: https://pitchfork.com/features/interview/7727-kraftwerk/. Accessed October 30, 2020.

Richter, M. (2021) 'Max Richter's songs to compel' *Take 5 Podcast*, ABC Classic FM. Broadcast 26 February 2021.

Schult, E. (2013), 'Emil Schult on Kraftwerk'. *Electronic Beats Magazine*. 24 November. Available at: www.electronicbeats.net/emil-schult-on-kraftwerk/ Accessed 1 March 2021.
Schütte, U. (2020), *Kraftwerk: Future Music from Germany*. London. Penguin Random House UK.
Stubbs, D. (2009), 'Kraftwerk', in N. Kotsopoulos (ed). *Krautrock: Cosmic Rock and It's Legacy*. London: Black Dog Publishing.
Stubbs, D. (2014), *Future Days: Krautrock and the Building of Modern Germany*. London. Faber and Faber.
Toltz, J. (2011), 'Dragged into the Dance' – The Role of Kraftwerk in the Development of Electro-Funk', in S. Albiez and D. Pattie (eds) *Kraftwerk: Music Non-Stop*. New York: The Continuum International Publishing Group.
Toop, D. (2003), 'Kraftwerk: sound in straight lines' *Dazed and Confused*, Vol. 2, No. 6.

Also available in the series

1. *Dusty Springfield's Dusty in Memphis* by Warren Zanes
2. *Love's Forever Changes* by Andrew Hultkrans
3. *Neil Young's Harvest* by Sam Inglis
4. *The Kinks' The Kinks Are the Village Green Preservation Society* by Andy Miller
5. *The Smiths' Meat Is Murder* by Joe Pernice
6. *Pink Floyd's The Piper at the Gates of Dawn* by John Cavanagh
7. *ABBA's ABBA Gold: Greatest Hits* by Elisabeth Vincentelli
8. *The Jimi Hendrix Experience's Electric Ladyland* by John Perry
9. *Joy Division's Unknown Pleasures* by Chris Ott
10. *Prince's Sign "☮" the Times* by Michaelangelo Matos
11. *The Velvet Underground's The Velvet Underground & Nico* by Joe Harvard
12. *The Beatles' Let It Be* by Steve Matteo
13. *James Brown's Live at the Apollo* by Douglas Wolk
14. *Jethro Tull's Aqualung* by Allan Moore
15. *Radiohead's OK Computer* by Dai Griffiths
16. *The Replacements' Let It Be* by Colin Meloy
17. *Led Zeppelin's Led Zeppelin IV* by Erik Davis

18. *The Rolling Stones' Exile on Main St.* by Bill Janovitz
19. *The Beach Boys' Pet Sounds* by Jim Fusilli
20. *Ramones' Ramones* by Nicholas Rombes
21. *Elvis Costello's Armed Forces* by Franklin Bruno
22. *R.E.M.'s Murmur* by J. Niimi
23. *Jeff Buckley's Grace* by Daphne Brooks
24. *DJ Shadow's Endtroducing. . . . .* by Eliot Wilder
25. *MC5's Kick Out the Jams* by Don McLeese
26. *David Bowie's Low* by Hugo Wilcken
27. *Bruce Springsteen's Born in the U.S.A.* by Geoffrey Himes
28. *The Band's Music from Big Pink* by John Niven
29. *Neutral Milk Hotel's In the Aeroplane over the Sea* by Kim Cooper
30. *Beastie Boys' Paul's Boutique* by Dan Le Roy
31. *Pixies' Doolittle* by Ben Sisario
32. *Sly and the Family Stone's There's a Riot Goin' On* by Miles Marshall Lewis
33. *The Stone Roses' The Stone Roses* by Alex Green
34. *Nirvana's In Utero* by Gillian G. Gaar
35. *Bob Dylan's Highway 61 Revisited* by Mark Polizzotti
36. *My Bloody Valentine's Loveless* by Mike McGonigal
37. *The Who's The Who Sell Out* by John Dougan
38. *Guided by Voices' Bee Thousand* by Marc Woodworth
39. *Sonic Youth's Daydream Nation* by Matthew Stearns
40. *Joni Mitchell's Court and Spark* by Sean Nelson
41. *Guns N' Roses' Use Your Illusion I and II* by Eric Weisbard
42. *Stevie Wonder's Songs in the Key of Life* by Zeth Lundy

43. *The Byrds' The Notorious Byrd Brothers* by Ric Menck
44. *Captain Beefheart's Trout Mask Replica* by Kevin Courrier
45. *Minutemen's Double Nickels on the Dime* by Michael T. Fournier
46. *Steely Dan's Aja* by Don Breithaupt
47. *A Tribe Called Quest's People's Instinctive Travels and the Paths of Rhythm* by Shawn Taylor
48. *PJ Harvey's Rid of Me* by Kate Schatz
49. *U2's Achtung Baby* by Stephen Catanzarite
50. *Belle & Sebastian's If You're Feeling Sinister* by Scott Plagenhoef
51. *Nick Drake's Pink Moon* by Amanda Petrusich
52. *Celine Dion's Let's Talk About Love* by Carl Wilson
53. *Tom Waits' Swordfishtrombones* by David Smay
54. *Throbbing Gristle's 20 Jazz Funk Greats* by Drew Daniel
55. *Patti Smith's Horses* by Philip Shaw
56. *Black Sabbath's Master of Reality* by John Darnielle
57. *Slayer's Reign in Blood* by D.X. Ferris
58. *Richard and Linda Thompson's Shoot Out the Lights* by Hayden Childs
59. *The Afghan Whigs' Gentlemen* by Bob Gendron
60. *The Pogues' Rum, Sodomy, and the Lash* by Jeffery T. Roesgen
61. *The Flying Burrito Brothers' The Gilded Palace of Sin* by Bob Proehl
62. *Wire's Pink Flag* by Wilson Neate
63. *Elliott Smith's XO* by Mathew Lemay
64. *Nas' Illmatic* by Matthew Gasteier
65. *Big Star's Radio City* by Bruce Eaton

66. *Madness' One Step Beyond. . .* by Terry Edwards
67. *Brian Eno's Another Green World* by Geeta Dayal
68. *The Flaming Lips' Zaireeka* by Mark Richardson
69. *The Magnetic Fields' 69 Love Songs* by LD Beghtol
70. *Israel Kamakawiwo'ole's Facing Future* by Dan Kois
71. *Public Enemy's It Takes a Nation of Millions to Hold Us Back* by Christopher R. Weingarten
72. *Pavement's Wowee Zowee* by Bryan Charles
73. *AC/DC's Highway to Hell* by Joe Bonomo
74. *Van Dyke Parks's Song Cycle* by Richard Henderson
75. *Slint's Spiderland* by Scott Tennent
76. *Radiohead's Kid A* by Marvin Lin
77. *Fleetwood Mac's Tusk* by Rob Trucks
78. *Nine Inch Nails' Pretty Hate Machine* by Daphne Carr
79. *Ween's Chocolate and Cheese* by Hank Shteamer
80. *Johnny Cash's American Recordings* by Tony Tost
81. *The Rolling Stones' Some Girls* by Cyrus Patell
82. *Dinosaur Jr.'s You're Living All Over Me* by Nick Attfield
83. *Television's Marquee Moon* by Bryan Waterman
84. *Aretha Franklin's Amazing Grace* by Aaron Cohen
85. *Portishead's Dummy* by RJ Wheaton
86. *Talking Heads' Fear of Music* by Jonathan Lethem
87. *Serge Gainsbourg's Histoire de Melody Nelson* by Darran Anderson
88. *They Might Be Giants' Flood* by S. Alexander Reed and Elizabeth Sandifer
89. *Andrew W.K.'s I Get Wet* by Phillip Crandall

90. *Aphex Twin's Selected Ambient Works Volume II* by Marc Weidenbaum
91. *Gang of Four's Entertainment* by Kevin J.H. Dettmar
92. *Richard Hell and the Voidoids' Blank Generation* by Pete Astor
93. *J Dilla's Donuts* by Jordan Ferguson
94. *The Beach Boys' Smile* by Luis Sanchez
95. *Oasis' Definitely Maybe* by Alex Niven
96. *Liz Phair's Exile in Guyville* by Gina Arnold
97. *Kanye West's My Beautiful Dark Twisted Fantasy* by Kirk Walker Graves
98. *Danger Mouse's The Grey Album* by Charles Fairchild
99. *Sigur Rós's ()* by Ethan Hayden
100. *Michael Jackson's Dangerous* by Susan Fast
101. *Can's Tago Mago* by Alan Warner
102. *Bobbie Gentry's Ode to Billie Joe* by Tara Murtha
103. *Hole's Live Through This* by Anwen Crawford
104. *Devo's Freedom of Choice* by Evie Nagy
105. *Dead Kennedys' Fresh Fruit for Rotting Vegetables* by Michael Stewart Foley
106. *Koji Kondo's Super Mario Bros.* by Andrew Schartmann
107. *Beat Happening's Beat Happening* by Bryan C. Parker
108. *Metallica's Metallica* by David Masciotra
109. *Phish's A Live One* by Walter Holland
110. *Miles Davis' Bitches Brew* by George Grella Jr.
111. *Blondie's Parallel Lines* by Kembrew McLeod
112. *Grateful Dead's Workingman's Dead* by Buzz Poole
113. *New Kids On The Block's Hangin' Tough* by Rebecca Wallwork

114. *The Geto Boys' The Geto Boys* by Rolf Potts
115. *Sleater-Kinney's Dig Me Out* by Jovana Babovic
116. *LCD Soundsystem's Sound of Silver* by Ryan Leas
117. *Donny Hathaway's Donny Hathaway Live* by Emily J. Lordi
118. *The Jesus and Mary Chain's Psychocandy* by Paula Mejia
119. *The Modern Lovers' The Modern Lovers* by Sean L. Maloney
120. *Angelo Badalamenti's Soundtrack from Twin Peaks* by Clare Nina Norelli
121. *Young Marble Giants' Colossal Youth* by Michael Blair and Joe Bucciero
122. *The Pharcyde's Bizarre Ride II the Pharcyde* by Andrew Barker
123. *Arcade Fire's The Suburbs* by Eric Eidelstein
124. *Bob Mould's Workbook* by Walter Biggins and Daniel Couch
125. *Camp Lo's Uptown Saturday Night* by Patrick Rivers and Will Fulton
126. *The Raincoats' The Raincoats* by Jenn Pelly
127. *Björk's Homogenic* by Emily Mackay
128. *Merle Haggard's Okie from Muskogee* by Rachel Lee Rubin
129. *Fugazi's In on the Kill Taker* by Joe Gross
130. *Jawbreaker's 24 Hour Revenge Therapy* by Ronen Givony
131. *Lou Reed's Transformer* by Ezra Furman
132. *Siouxsie and the Banshees' Peepshow* by Samantha Bennett
133. *Drive-By Truckers' Southern Rock Opera* by Rien Fertel
134. *dc Talk's Jesus Freak* by Will Stockton and D. Gilson
135. *Tori Amos's Boys for Pele* by Amy Gentry
136. *Odetta's One Grain of Sand* by Matthew Frye Jacobson

137. *Manic Street Preachers' The Holy Bible* by David Evans
138. *The Shangri-Las' Golden Hits of the Shangri-Las* by Ada Wolin
139. *Tom Petty's Southern Accents* by Michael Washburn
140. *Massive Attack's Blue Lines* by Ian Bourland
141. *Wendy Carlos's Switched-On Bach* by Roshanak Kheshti
142. *The Wild Tchoupitoulas' The Wild Tchoupitoulas* by Bryan Wagner
143. *David Bowie's Diamond Dogs* by Glenn Hendler
144. *D'Angelo's Voodoo* by Faith A. Pennick
145. *Judy Garland's Judy at Carnegie Hall* by Manuel Betancourt
146. *Elton John's Blue Moves* by Matthew Restall
147. *Various Artists' I'm Your Fan: The Songs of Leonard Cohen* by Ray Padgett
148. *Janet Jackson's The Velvet Rope* by Ayanna Dozier
149. *Suicide's Suicide* by Andi Coulter
150. *Elvis Presley's From Elvis in Memphis* by Eric Wolfson
151. *Nick Cave and the Bad Seeds' Murder Ballads* by Santi Elijah Holley
152. *24 Carat Black's Ghetto: Misfortune's Wealth* by Zach Schonfeld
153. *Carole King's Tapestry* by Loren Glass
154. *Pearl Jam's Vs.* by Clint Brownlee
155. *Roxy Music's Avalon* by Simon Morrison
156. *Duran Duran's Rio* by Annie Zaleski
157. *Donna Summer's Once Upon a Time* by Alex Jeffery
158. *Sam Cooke's Live at the Harlem Square Club, 1963* by Colin Fleming
159. *Janelle Monáe's The ArchAndroid* by Alyssa Favreau

160. *John Prine's John Prine* by Erin Osmon
161. *Maria Callas's Lyric and Coloratura Arias* by Ginger Dellenbaugh
162. *The National's Boxer* by Ryan Pinkard
163. *Kraftwerk's Computer World* by Steve Tupai Francis